Alaska's Great Interior

Volume 7, Number 1 / 1980 / Alaska Geographic®

The Alaska Geographic Society

To teach many more to better know and use our natural resources

ABOUT THIS ISSUE:

Alaska's Great Interior is primarily the work of Interior residents—writers and photographers who responded to our call for submissions with some excellent material.

Four well-known Interior writers stand out for their contributions: Tom Walker wrote our *Land Between the Mountains* introduction; Jo Anne Wold contributed *History: From Bark Canoes to Gas Pipelines;* Jane Pender offered two articles— *Fairbanks Today* and an interesting sidebar, *Usibelli Coal: Power and Energy at Healy*—and Pat Monaghan profiled some lively *People of the Interior.*

Our thanks to all who helped tackle this, the largest region of Alaska we have attempted to cover in our *ALASKA GEOGRAPHIC®* series.

Editor's note: Community and village populations are the most recent figures available at press time from the Fairbanks North Star Borough and the Tanana Chiefs Conference. Most of the figures are compiled from a count made in the summer 1978. For Fairbanks and larger neighboring communities, 1979 figures are given.

Editors: Robert A. Henning, Marty Loken, Barbara Olds
Associate Editor: Penny Rennick
Editorial Assistance: Robert N. De Armond, Tim Jones
Designer: Dianne Hofbeck
Cartographer: Jon.Hersh

ALASKA GEOGRAPHIC®, ISSN 0361-1353, is published quarterly by The Alaska Geographic Society, Anchorage, AK 99509-3370. Second-class postage paid in Anchorage, AK 99509. Printed in Thailand.

THE ALASKA GEOGRAPHIC SOCIETY is a nonprofit organization exploring new frontiers of knowledge across the lands of the polar rim, learning how other men and other countries live in their Norths, putting the geography book back in the classroom, exploring new methods of teaching and learning—sharing in the excitement of discovery in man's wonderful new world north of 51°16'.

MEMBERS OF THE SOCIETY RECEIVE *Alaska Geographic®,* a quality magazine in color which devotes each quarterly issue to monographic in-depth coverage of a northern geographic region or resource-oriented subject.

MEMBERSHIP DUES in The Alaska Geographic Society are $39 per year. (Eighty percent of each year's dues is for a one-year subscription to *Alaska Geographic®.*) Order from The Alaska Geographic Society, Box 93370, Anchorage, AK 99509; (907) 258-2515.

MATERIAL SOUGHT: The editors of *Alaska Geographic®* seek a wide variety of informative material on the lands north of 51°16' on geographic subjects—anything to do with resources and their uses (with heavy emphasis on quality color photography)—from Alaska, Northern Canada, Siberia, Japan—all geographic areas that have a relationship to Alaska in a physical or economic sense. In early 1980 editors were seeking material on the following geographic regions and subjects: Wrangell-St. Elias Mountains, the Kobuk-Noatak area, and glaciers of Alaska. We do not want material done in excessive scientific terminology. A query to the editors is suggested. Payments are made for all material upon publication.

Library of Congress Cataloging in Publication Data
Main entry under title:
Alaska's great interior.
    (Alaska geographic; v. 7, no. 1 ISSN 0361-1353)
    CONTENTS: Walker, T. Land between the mountains.—Wold, J.A. History.—Along the rivers.—Along the highways. [etc.]
    1. Alaska—Description and travel—1959-
—Addresses, essays, lectures.   2. Fairbanks, Alaska—Description—Addresses, essays, lectures.   I. Henning, Robert A.   II. Loken, Marty.   III. Olds, Barbara.   IV. Series.
F901.A266 vol. 7, no. 1 [F905]   979.8'6   79-25381
ISBN 0-88240-138-6

The cover—Terrain in the Interior is a combination of mountains, taiga and tundra. This photo of Monohan Flat, with fireweed in the foreground and the Alaska Range in the background, shows the lay of the land.
(Charlie Ott, reprinted from *ALASKA®* magazine)

Previous page—The John River, formed by the confluence of Contact and Inukpasugruk creeks, meanders south for 125 miles from Anaktuvuk Pass in the Brooks Range to enter the Koyukuk River near Bettles.
(George Wuerthner)

Right—Stands of aspen cover many slopes of the Interior. Other principal trees are black and white spruce, paper birch, balsam poplar, black cottonwood, western larch and tamarack.
(Ed Cooper)

"The Interior"

has, to us, always been a term loaded with exciting promise. To leave the coast and go back into the land beyond the mountains has to many Eskimos and Indians been through history a frequent excursion into danger among unfriendly foes, sometimes into a land peopled by spirits. Still, from time to time, coastal Natives dared to go into the "Interior" in pursuit of game, fish, fur, sometimes for trade, often out of driving curiosity.

Today, the excitement of wondering what adventures, what treasures, what sights lie behind the coastal ranges still is a real thing to us. And there are treasures and wonderful sights and adventures today. For many who live in this heartland of Alaska (some refer to Fairbanks as The Golden Heart City, a much more apt description in years past when there were great gold dredges scooping away on every hand) there is a special charm. Here birch and poplar lie in gentle folds over rolling hills and across wide flatlands carved by meandering rivers. The harsher peaks of surrounding mountain ranges are low in the blue haze of distance. There is a musky perfume of lingonberries, blueberries, Hudson's Bay tea and spruce. Sometimes, in the heat haze of June, our memory-nose also recalls the sharp pungent odor of citronella, for this is a place where man and insects wage a ceaseless battle. And temperatures themselves challenge man here—100 above to 70 below. Shortness of seasons—a long dark winter and a furiously paced summer are the dominant times. Spring, which comes so suddenly leaves burst from the trees in a matter of days almost before the ice has ceased running in

the miracle of breakup. Fall is only a few weeks of browning hilltops and a great golden aura of dying leaves.

Here behind the mountains there is little wind. Smoke stands stiffly over chimneys, as if frozen in the below zero air. Puffballs of layered dry powder snow balance unwaveringly on the fence posts. In the summer one's feet crunch in the dry tundra or scattered twigs of the forest floor. In winter steps squeak on the trail and on the city streets made foggy dim by ice crystals and chimneys and auto exhausts.

A quiet land. The brush and the timber and the great distances muffle bird and animal sounds. The rivers, for the most part snakelike and muddy, make a rustling sound barely heard as the silt-laden current moves by the hulls of boats, the creak of a slowly turning fish wheel almost an apologetic sound not intended to break the spell.

And such a big land. Here you can truly see forever.

This, then, is the essence of "The Great Interior." There is much detail we must dwell on more at a later date, but here for starters is your introduction to yet another part of Alaska in the continuing effort of your Alaska Geographic Society to help you to better know our land.

Sincerely,

Robert A. Henning

President
The Alaska Geographic Society

The Tanana River and mountains of the Alaska Range, photographed on a summer day with arctic poppies brightening the foreground.
(Ed Cooper)

Land
Between the Mountains

*T*he Great Interior, an area spread across almost one-third of Alaska, yet home to less than 20% of its people, is largely wilderness—little changed by man and still the home of the grizzly, peregrine falcon and wolf. Defining the Interior can be a difficult task; we could describe the region in political, ethnic, economic or geographic terms . . . and each description would be different. Let's start with a general geographic description.

Beginning at the Alaska-Yukon border where the Alaska Highway enters the state, the Interior's southern boundary heads northwest, paralleling the road to the village of Tok. From there, the line follows the crest of the Alaska Range in its arcing path to Rainy Pass, northwest of Anchorage and southwest of 20,320-foot Mount McKinley. From there the border becomes somewhat arbitrary, sweeping northwest past McGrath and Nulato, then arcing northeast to follow the divide of the Brooks Range to the Alaska-Yukon border, the Interior's eastern boundary.

Generally, this description is based on river drainages, centering around major tributaries of the Yukon River above Kaltag. The Yukon itself, the state's longest river, flows 1,400 miles through Alaska and another 475 miles through Canada. This description includes the state's second-longest river, the 555-mile Porcupine; the third-longest, the 554-mile Koyukuk; the fifth-longest, the 531-mile Tanana; and the tenth-longest, the 314-mile Birch Creek. The Interior also encompasses the headwaters of the fourth-longest river, the 540-mile Kuskokwim.

The topography of Central Alaska is dominated by two great mountain ranges. The Brooks Range to the

*The topography
of Central Alaska
is dominated
by two great
mountain ranges.
The Brooks Range
to the north, and
the jagged-spired,
glacier-hung
Alaska Range
to the south . . .*

Arrigetch Valley, in Gates of the Arctic National Monument, with the spectacular Arrigetch Peaks in the background. The first snows of fall had recently fallen when this photo was taken in September.
(John and Margaret Ibbotson)

north, and the jagged-spired, glacier-hung Alaska Range in the south, limit and define this 165,000-square-mile region, an area slightly larger than California. The mountains on the north effectively seal off the region from the arctic climatic zone and the southern mountains shield it from the maritime zone. The continental climatic zone of the Interior is characterized by low precipitation—10 to 20 inches annually—stagnant air masses and extreme seasonal variations in temperature. The highest temperature ever recorded in Alaska was 100°F at Fort Yukon on June 27, 1915, and the lowest temperature, minus 80°F, was recorded at Prospect Creek on January 23, 1971. (The average temperature at Prospect that January was -51.9°F.)

About 60 miles northwest of Mount McKinley in the general area of Lake Minchumina is the geographic center of Alaska, 63°50' north, 152° west. The Interior's climate, then, is primarily the effect of latitude. The Arctic Circle sweeps through the region. The summer sun shines almost 24 hours a day but is nearly absent in winter. Fairbanks has a summer maximum of 21 hours, 49 minutes of daylight, and a winter minimum of 3 hours, 42 minutes. The first frost

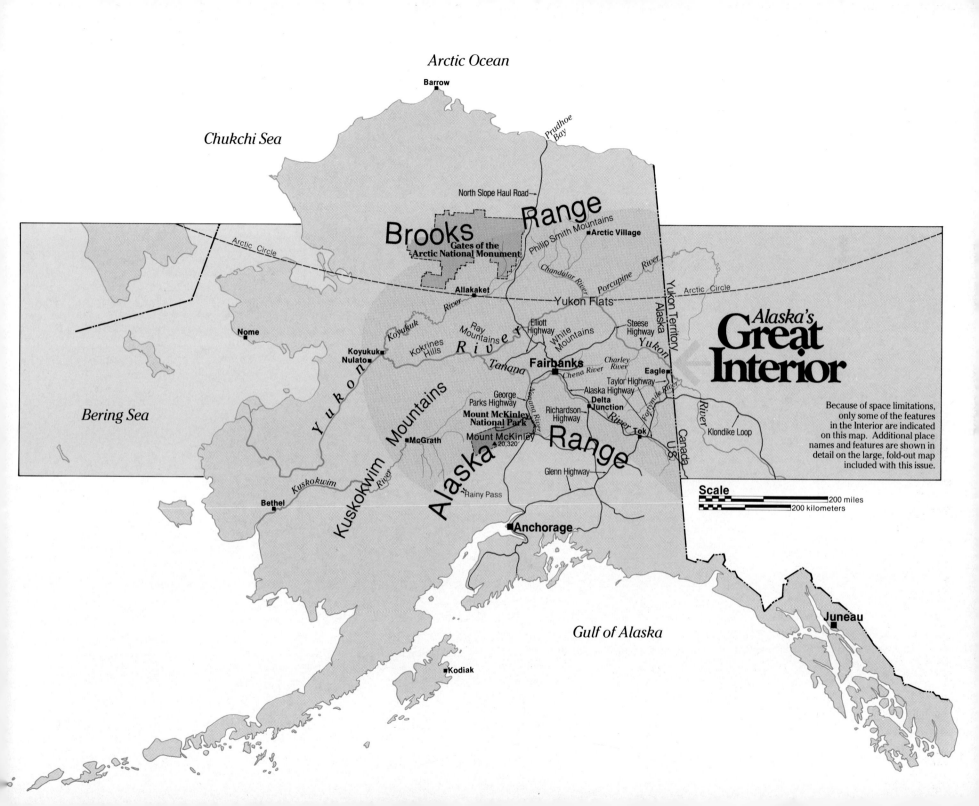

typically arrives in September and much of the land stays frozen until early May, although frosts into June are not uncommon in some spots. The area around Delta Junction has, on the mean, only 114 consecutive days when the temperature stays above freezing, a regional high. The Koyukuk River at Hughes (population 100), freezes up in mid-October and generally doesn't thaw until mid-May, remaining frozen seven full months.

Just as the heights of the Brooks and Alaska ranges influence the Interior's overall climatic conditions, terrain and altitude alter local patterns. The Kuskokwim Mountains, Ray Mountains, Philip Smith Mountains and the Tanana Hills-White Mountains are important highlands. These ranges, with peaks to 6,800 feet, pale in comparison to the sky-scraping Alaska Range, but are important climatologically and otherwise.

The mountain ranges screen lowlands and these protected areas are both the coldest and warmest areas in the Interior. Fort Yukon (population 700), shows recorded temperature extremes of 100°F, the state high, and a low of -75°F. High winds are relatively infrequent and the masses of stagnant air combine with the lack of solar heating to permit winter temperatures to reach extreme lows for extended periods. Records for Eielson Air Force Base show that the wind is calm an average of 41% of the time (55% in winter), contrasted with Galena (population 631), where the wind is calm only 13% of the time.

The central Interior has a high winter pollution

Opposite
The Kuskokwim Mountains between Flat and McGrath. The range is 430 miles long and 50 miles wide and takes its name from the Kuskokwim River, which flows across the range.
(Jerry Hout)

Left
Early prospectors had the right idea in naming the White Mountains north of Fairbanks. Composed of white limestone, these snow-covered slopes retain their whiteness year-round.
(Kenneth R. Kollodge)

On this December 29th, the temperature plummeted to -44°F outside a snow-covered cabin along the Yukon River at Fort Yukon.
(Gil Mull)

potential. Air pollution requires three things: proper terrain, air conditions favorable to formation and a source. The Interior's river valleys, basins, and lowlands are ideal terrain for air pollution. As a winter high pressure system settles over the region, the skies clear and without clouds to slow heat loss, the air at ground level cools and an inversion forms. Under normal conditions, air is warmest at ground level, cooling off with altitude. In an inversion, temperatures are reversed, with the coldest temperatures at ground level, warmer temperatures at altitude. The absence of vertical mixing within an inversion layer permits pollution to concentrate instead of being lifted upward to be carried away by winds aloft. An inversion acts as a lid on a natural bowl to hold in the pollution. The strongest, most persistent inversions in the world, fully three times stronger than those over Los Angeles, occur over Fairbanks (population 24,641 within the city limits), in the Tanana Valley.

Ice fog forms during cold weather of -25°F, or lower, and is produced when water vapor is discharged into the super-cooled air, freezing into large ice crystals. Natural sources of ice fog are the hot springs common to the Interior, rapid moving streams that stay ice free year-round and overflows. The phenomenon becomes acute, and dangerous, in communities when ice crystals form around particles discharged into the air by vehicle exhaust, from home and business heating units and community power plants. In Fairbanks in winter, the air quality problem is critical because the pollutants are being produced at peak levels to cope with the extreme cold, and are

Ice fog forms when
temperatures descend to -25°F
or lower and water vapor
discharged into super-cooled
air freezes into large ice
crystals. The top photo, taken
at -40°F, shows housing at the
University of Alaska with
Fairbanks in the background
hidden under a layer of ice fog.
The bottom photo, taken
from the same location,
shows the city with the
temperature at +9°F.
(Both photos by Tom Walker)

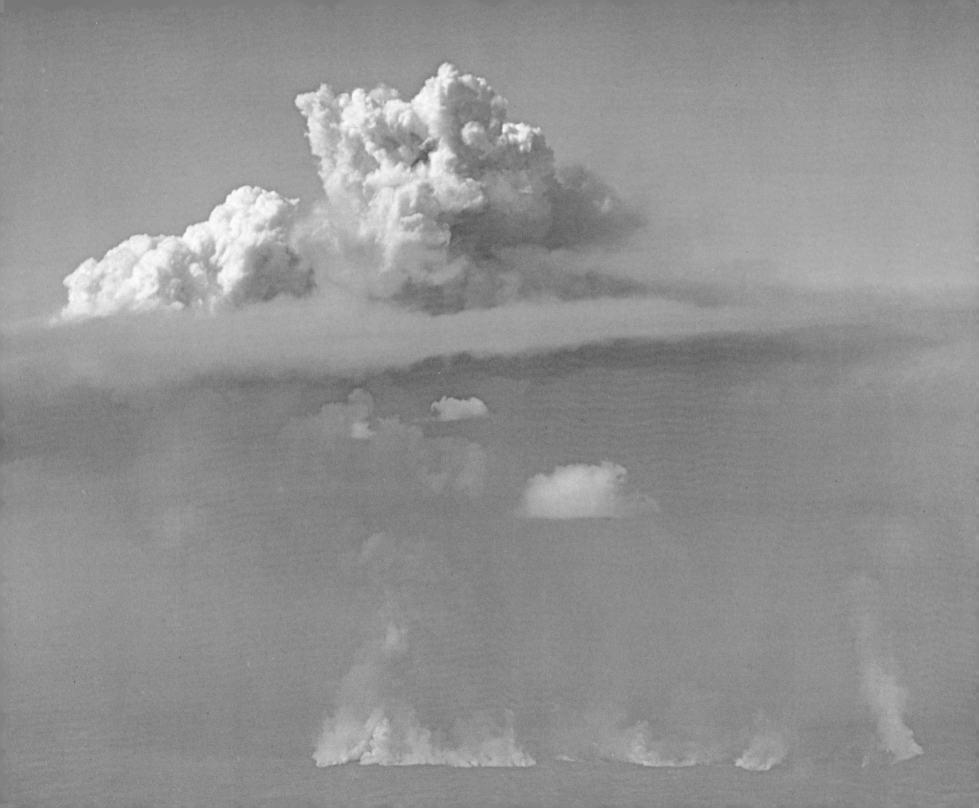

concentrated, with little or no dispersion, by the inversions. The layer of ice fog can be anywhere from 30 to 60 feet thick during critical periods and can exceed federal air pollution standards.

Air pollution from wildfires is common in summer. Over the past 10 years, wildfires have burned an average of half a million acres in the Interior. Low precipitation and long hours of summer sunlight combine to make the ground cover highly flammable, and smoke-hazy days are a fact of summer life. Most fires are caused by lightning and man's carelessness. Such fires keep millions of acres of commercial forest land in immature successional stages. Wildfire suppression on some noncommercial forest lands may not be as important, or as necessary as once believed. The regrowth on burned-over land provides excellent habitat for many wildlife species, including moose, hares and ptarmigan. Where possible, some resource managers favor allowing forest and tundra fires to run their natural course.

The tundra (Russian for treeless) can burn as easily as forest land. There are two types of tundra—moist or wet, usually found in the Arctic above tree line but also common to the foothills of the Alaska and Brooks ranges, and dry or alpine, found on ridges and rubble slopes from 2,000 to 4,000 feet. Wet tundra is a variable, low-growing plant community with a nearly continuous ground cover of dwarf birch, willows, blueberries, sedges, grasses, lichens and various wild flowers. In contrast, alpine tundra is characterized by sparse vegetation with plants seldom more than a few inches high. Wild flowers, such as mountain avens, along with a few grasses and lichens predominate on dry tundra. Above 4,500 feet, except for a few flowering plants and rock lichens, most mountains are bare.

Tundra is the least productive of Alaska's biotic subdivisions, and the slowest to recover from damage. The growing season is short, 45 to 90 days, so lichens, an important caribou food, are extremely slow growing, adding as little as one inch of new growth every five years, requiring 30 to 50 years to recover from overgrazing.

Left
Air pollution from wildfires is common in the summer. Over the past 10 years, fires have burned an average of half a million acres in the Interior. This fire is burning near the Salt River north of Fairbanks. (Myron Wright)

Clockwise from below
► Mountain avens or eight-petaled dryas. (Charlie Ott)
► Areas with cool temperatures, frequent winds and moisture-retaining soils support a form of vegetation known as tundra. As this photo taken near Walker Lake shows, tundra includes a variety of flowers, mosses and lichens. (Charlotte Casey, Staff)
► Alaska cotton or cotton grass may grow to two feet and is common near tundra ponds. Alaska cotton makes a beautiful, long-lasting bouquet if picked before the seeds ripen. (Charlie Ott)

15

The boreal forest, or taiga (Russian for "Land of Little Sticks"), densely covers most highlands and river valleys below 2,000 feet. Hillside stands of white spruce, birch and aspen give way on wet muskeg areas to scattered thickets of scraggly black spruce, which can be over 200 years old but only six to eight feet tall. Dominant trees are the black and white spruce, paper birch, quaking aspen, balsam poplar, black cottonwood, western larch and tamarack, a deciduous conifer. Common shrubs are labrador tea, prickly rose, willow, alder, numerous berries, flowers, wild grasses and sedges.

The Interior is not usually thought of as prime commercial forest land, but of Alaska's 28.2 million acres

latitudes. Logging and commercial use of Interior wood products have been on a minor scale to date, with some timber harvested for local consumption as rough-cut and dimensional lumber and building logs, and with a small amount of pulp wood sent to Japan. Most acreage remains untouched because of its inaccessibility.

All of Interior lies within the discontinuous permafrost zone, where permafrost varies from continuous in the north to discontinuous in the south with some south-sloping hillsides and river plains permafrost-free. Permafrost is ground that has remained frozen for at least two years in succession, although much of it has been in existence for tens of thousands of years,

Hillside stands of white spruce, birch and aspen give way on wet muskeg areas to scattered thickets of scraggly black spruce, which can be over 200 years old . . .

classed as commercial forest, 22.5 million acres are in the Interior, with an inventory estimate of 30.8 billion board feet. The three main commercially valuable species are white spruce, aspen and birch. The most valuable is the white spruce which grows best on warm, dry, south-facing hillsides with good drainage and no permafrost. White spruce can grow to 80 feet and have 15-inch (or bigger) diameters.

White spruce predominates over 12.8 million acres of the Interior and produces medium-grade lumber and pulp chips, while aspen and birch are primarily pulp sources. Studies at Bonanza Creek Experimental Forest, west of Fairbanks, have shown that it takes 100 to 150 years to grow saw timber in the Interior, with natural reseeding much slower than in lower

as evidenced by occasional finds of the frozen remains of mammoths and other ice-age animals. Dating of Interior permafrost has placed it at 14,000 to 32,000 years old.

Interior highlands are well drained and nearly plant bare, while lower hillsides are covered with heavy forest, tapering to stunted spruce on the swampy flatlands. Potholes and ponds dot the land, while countless small watercourses wind toward the rivers that drain the region. Most waterways meander aimlessly with old oxbows and sloughs too numerous to count. These ponds, marshes and swamps are indicators of the underlying permafrost, a barrier to water percolation into the ground.

Despite low annual precipitation, flooding, partially

The Yukon River works its way through the bluffs of the Yukon-Tanana highlands near Woodchopper Creek in the eastern Interior.
(Gil Mull)

attributable to permafrost, is a recurring problem. The 1967 flood which inundated Fairbanks and Nenana (population 508), was the result of abnormally heavy rain (six inches in six days) and rapid runoff. The saturated soils quickly shed the water causing record high water along the Chena and Tanana flood plain. The Chena River Lakes Flood Control Project is being constructed by the U.S. Army Corps of Engineers as a hedge against future flooding. Each year along the Yukon and its tributaries, villages are flooded or lose riverbank dwellings to high water and erosion.

The Yukon River basin may have the greatest electric-generating potential in North America, but at the moment there are no hydroelectric plants in the Interior. The proposed Rampart Canyon Dam on the Yukon River, a project that would have formed a 10,850-square-mile lake, was determined in 1971 by the Corps of Engineers to be uneconomical and has been shelved for the foreseeable future. No fewer than 18 hydroelectric sites have been identified in the area, involving the Yukon, Koyukuk, Nenana, Tanana, Porcupine and Fortymile rivers, with four major dams proposed. Currently some local communities get their electrical energy from small diesel-powered or coal-fired generators.

Each year, attracted by the region's numerous lakes, rivers and wetlands, millions of ducks, geese, swans and cranes arrive from southern wintering grounds to breed and raise their young. The Tanana, Porcupine, lower Koyukuk, and Yukon river basins are extremely productive waterfowl habitats. From the 11,000-square-mile Yukon Flats, containing almost 2.5 million acres of waterfowl habitat, nearly 2.2 million ducks and geese fly south each fall. Mallards, pintails, American widgeons, lesser scaups, green-winged teals, northern shovelers and canvasbacks are the predominant species nesting in the Interior. A few trumpeter and whistling swans also nest there as do numbers of lesser Canada and white-fronted geese. Sandhill cranes, common and arctic loons, and divers, such as grebes and goldeneyes, also nest in the Interior.

Interior wetlands attract many species of migrant shorebirds, notably golden plovers, spotted sandpipers and dunlins, yellowlegs and phalaropes. Herring, mew and Bonaparte's gulls; Arctic terns and long-tailed jaegers also are common in the region. Some are champion fliers; the Arctic tern comes from as far away as the tip of South America or Antarctica, and the golden plover arrives from the Galapagos Islands.

Flooding has been a problem for many communities along the rivers of the Interior. Part of the Chena River Lakes Flood Control Project is this facility at Moose Creek, 20 miles east of Fairbanks.
(Mark Kelley)

Minto Flats, some 130 miles northwest of Fairbanks, photographed from the new village of Minto. This is prime waterfowl habitat and serves as a breeding ground for several species of the Interior's water birds.
(June Mackie)

Millions of small birds also come north to breed and nest, the wheatear being the record long-distance migrant, coming from Africa, a distance of 5,000 miles. Lapland longspurs, snow buntings, several varieties of finches, thrushes, warblers, blackbirds, sparrows, juncos and crossbills also come north to rear their young in the short summer.

Just as the birds come north to take advantage of the aquatic habitat and raise their young on the abundant insect life, (the mosquito being Alaska's most numerous form of wildlife), many predatory birds in turn prey upon the teeming summer flocks. Twenty species of raptors have been identified in the Interior, 18 of which nest there. A few bald eagles nest along

river valleys, while some golden eagles nest in alpine areas. Ospreys, goshawks, red-tailed hawks, marsh hawks, American kestrels and great horned owls are widely distributed. A few gyrfalcons may nest in the southern Interior, while the endangered peregrine falcon nests along the Yukon and Charley rivers, and elsewhere. The short-eared owl, boreal owl, hawk owl, great gray owl, and perhaps the snowy owl, also nest in the region.

Very few bird species remain year-round in the Interior. Ravens, Gray jays, grosbeaks and chickadees are the main year-round residents with an occasional common flicker and hairy or downy woodpecker. Many predators also go south in winter, most notably

Left
The male rock ptarmigan in winter plumage can be distinguished from the other two species of ptarmigan, the willow and white-tailed, by the black bar through its eye. Rock ptarmigan frequent higher and more rocky ground than willow ptarmigan. Winter flocks move from place to place in search of food during most of the daylight hours. Rock ptarmigan must eat the equivalent of one-tenth to one-fifth of their body weight each day.
(Stephen Krasemann)

Above
The common loon, one of several varieties of waterfowl that nest in the wetlands of the Interior. All four species of North American loons have been recorded in Mount McKinley National Park.
(Jim Shives)

Below
Conspicuous black-and-white markings denote the snow bunting, a common perching bird of the Interior.
(Doug Murphy)

Left
Long, pointed wings, a forked tail, black cap and bright red bill distinguish the Arctic tern, a long-distance flyer that summers in the Interior and winters in the Antarctic.
(Brad Ebel)

the peregrine falcon which follows its prey, the waterfowl, to the lower states. Game birds such as the ruffed, spruce and sharp-tailed grouse and willow and rock ptarmigan stay throughout the year, but migrate from winter to summer range. Populations of grouse and ptarmigan vary from extreme scarcity to fantastic abundance.

During the short northern summer the land is alive with wildlife, giving the impression of teeming life. Yet, when winter comes, the land empties except for a few hardy species. On a per-acre basis, northern habitats are poor wildlife producers. The seasonal cycles of migratory birds are paralleled by the broader cycling of mammal populations. Many

23

Left
Following a peak population in 1971, snowshoe hares are now recovering from a major decline in their numbers in the Interior. Characteristically, these animals fluctuate in numbers on a 10-year cycle. Populations may be as dense as 2,000 to 3,000 hares per square mile during a peak year, and as low as 1 to 50 per square mile a few years later.
(Stephen Krasemann)

Above
The wily fox is common throughout the Interior. Here a cross fox (a color phase of the red fox) sneaks up on prey in Mount McKinley National Park.
(June Mackie)

Right
Ranging over 50 miles in search of snowshoe hares or other small game, the lynx is an agile tree climber and a good swimmer. Its broad, well-furred feet act as snowshoes for easy winter travel.
(Tom Walker)

species, such as the lemming and snowshoe hare, follow predictable patterns of population highs and lows. The snowshoe hare cycles from a low to an extreme high every 10 to 12 years. The population dynamics of these important prey species also affect and are intertwined with fluctuations in predator populations. The Canada lynx is extremely dependent on hares and their numbers increase or decrease in direct relationship to the snowshoe hare population. Foxes and coyotes, as well as hawks and owls, are also dependent on hare and rodent populations. When hares are at low cycle, so are the predator populations.

Common Interior fur bearers are muskrats, beavers, otters, mink, marten, ermine, foxes, coyotes, lynx, wolves and wolverines. Each year trappers harvest an estimated $6 million worth of furs.

Interior big game animals are also somewhat cyclic, or at least in some cases closely tied to predator population fluctuations. Moose during the 1970's were at low levels in the Interior, theoretically as a result of high wolf predation, a series of harsh winters and overhunting. Some biologists point out that fire-suppression, which keeps forests in climax condition, might play a part in that the best moose habitat is the by-product of uncontrolled forest fire. Wolf populations are moderately high and are occasionally 'controlled' by aerial hunting.

Caribou, in four main herds (Beaver Mountains, Delta, McKinley and Porcupine), are at low levels in the Interior, with the exception of the 150,000-animal Porcupine herd, the state's largest. Numerous theories have been offered explaining the decline. The situation is not clearly understood however, although a variety of factors—natural cycles, predation, range condition and hunting—may be working

Beavers have a transparent covering over their eyes, and large hind feet, both of which are excellent adaptations to their aquatic lifestyle.
(Martin Grosnick)

25

Below
Barley, one of the key crops for the Delta barley project. In spite of a short Delta-area growing season of 90 to 120 days, the long hours of daylight there make the potential for photosynthesis the highest of any agricultural area in the world. Past production has yielded 60 bushels of barley per acre, 40% more than the average yield in the Lower 48. The protein content of Lower 48 barley is 9% to 11%. In Alaska, under good growing conditions, field-grown barley can reach protein contents of 10% to 16%, and under special test conditions, 21%.
(Sabra McCracken)

Right
Near the University of Alaska, just outside Fairbanks, is an experimental farm where this harvester is cutting grain.
(Tom Walker)

Below
Agriculture in bush Alaska is encouraged through various programs including the Extension Service of the University of Alaska. Experiments are being conducted in Galena, Ruby, Huslia and Allakaket. John Quirk, director of the program in Galena, holds some of the potatoes which grew to the tune of 10⅓ tons per acre.
(Matthew Donohoe)

Agriculture in the Interior

The total land area of Alaska is approximately 375 million acres, of which 1.6 million acres were listed as land in farms in the 1974 U.S. Census of Agriculture. Most of the land in farms consists of grazing land leased from the state or federal government. Excluding the large grazing areas, approximately 138,000 acres are included in land in farms. Slightly over 20,000 acres yield harvestable crops; the balance is in pasture and uncleared land. The number of farms in Alaska peaked in 1939 and had declined to an estimated 300 by 1979.

The Tanana Valley is the major agricultural area of the Interior and the only area of commercial agriculture north of the Alaska Range. Throughout the region there are a few pockets of local agricultural activity but these products are grown for home consumption or for trading.

In 1978 the total value of production in the Tanana Valley was $1,874,900. Crop value was $996,100; livestock and poultry value was $381,600. The chief horticulture crops for the valley are potatoes, cabbage, carrots, head lettuce and other lettuce, radishes, greenhouse tomatoes, cucumbers, zucchini, broccoli and cauliflower. The major field crops, including products from the Big Delta area, which is part of the Tanana Valley, are oats, barley, grassland hay and mixed grains. At this time the value of rapeseed production is minimal. In addition, livestock and poultry add to the commercial value of agriculture in the area. For the past few years there has been very little dairy activity in the Interior but this aspect of farming is now coming back and may play a role in commercial agriculture in the future. ☐

together to cause the decline. Caribou, unlike moose, are migratory and can move great distances to calve or find winter range.

Dall sheep are found in large numbers throughout the Alaska and Brooks ranges, and appear to be at a high and healthy population level. Small isolated bands of sheep are found in the Tanana Hills-White Mountains. Dall sheep, like moose, were heavily hunted for meat by market hunters at the turn of the century and many gold camps were kept well-supplied at the expense of the bands.

Bison were transplanted from Montana to the area around Delta Junction in June 1928 and the original 23-animal herd has grown to about 300. The animals live primarily on the grassy flats of the Delta and Gerstle rivers, moving, to the consternation of farmers, to the barley fields near Delta in early fall. In 1965 bison from the Delta herd were transplanted to the South Fork of the Kuskokwim to form the nucleus for a Farewell herd. Alaska Department of Fish & Game personnel recommend that this herd not exceed 100 animals.

A cow and calf moose. Populations of moose in the Interior are currently struggling with the loss of prime habitat, the new growth of willows and other shrubs which spring up after a forest fire. (Paul Andert)

Brown/grizzly and black bear are common in the Interior. Bears are omnivorous, feeding primarily on berries, various plants, small mammals and carrion. Occasionally bears kill big game, usually young, but more often are found feeding on the salmon that spawn in the many Interior rivers and streams.

King, silver and chum salmon spawn in the Interior. Kings and chums are found in most Yukon tributaries, while silvers are more restricted, spawning mostly in the Tanana drainage. Chums run twice each year, summer and fall, and these are the longest spawning runs known for this fish. Chums, like kings, travel up the Porcupine and Yukon well into the Yukon Territory. Chum runs of 10 million fish have been recorded, and provide protein for both people and animals. Each year tens of thousands of salmon are caught in nets and fish wheels for commercial and subsistence use.

Sport fishing is popular in the Interior. Salmon, grayling, arctic char, burbot, northern pike, lake trout and several species of whitefish (including sheefish) are the leading sport fish. Many also are caught for subsistence, with grayling, pike and whitefish being the most important. Fishing is good, but many waters are susceptible to overfishing. Most lakes are less productive than similar-sized waters in lower latitudes. Poor productivity is caused by the short growing season, minimal habitat due to the fact that some lakes occasionally freeze to the bottom and to oxygen levels that are below fish tolerance levels, a result of prolonged ice cover. Interior fish get large only because of low fishing pressure.

Interior waterways served the Athabascans not only as a source of protein, but as routes of travel, trade and exploration. In the early 1870's a few white

Left
The monarch of the Interior's animal kingdom is the brown/grizzly bear. This huge carnivore feeds on berries, squirrels, hoofed mammals, black bears and just about anything else it can find. In some areas of the Interior 100 square miles are needed to support one bear. (Myron Wright)

Clockwise from right
► One of the largest lakes in the Interior, Lake Minchumina is near the geographic center of Alaska, 66 miles northwest of Mount McKinley. The lake has a modest settlement where this fisherman, who has just landed a large pike, lives. (Don and Afton Blanc)
► A fishing boat is pulled upstream along the Yukon River at Circle. (John and Margaret Ibbotson)
► The grayling . . . delicious eating and one of the most sought-after of the Interior's sport fish. (Tom Walker)

men entered the region in search of furs and gold. They included Arthur Harper, Jack McQuesten and Al Mayo, all of whom remained in the country. Then in the 1880's, gold was found on the Fortymile River and more white men arrived. The discovery of gold in the Birch Creek district in 1894 brought about the founding of Circle, the first mining town of the Interior. It was the Klondike discovery of 1896, however, that brought the first real gold rush and lured more than 50,000 gold seekers north. A few disillusioned prospectors, not finding their pot of gold in Yukon Territory, trickled down the Yukon and ascended its tributaries. A wild rush to the Nome strike of 1898 brought still more prospectors into the country, eventually making strikes at Mastodon, Bonanza, Eureka, Stampede, Ophir, Nolan and Cripple creeks, and establishing such villages as Ruby, Kantishna, Wiseman, Manley, Livengood, Eagle and Rampart. However, it wasn't until 1902 when Felix Pedro made his strike north of the confluence of the Chena and Tanana rivers that the real gold bonanza of the region was found. Since that time the placer fields north of Fairbanks, near Ester and Pedro domes, have produced more than eight million ounces of gold. Gold production has been low the last 20 years but the decontrol of the gold price in the 1970's has spurred renewed interest in mining. In 1924, mostly as an adjunct to mining activities, the government built a railroad from the port of Seward to Fairbanks, ending the traditional dependence on river transport.

Mercury, antimony, platinum, tin, silver, lead, tungsten and molybdenum were mined in varying degrees through World War II. Some antimony and silver is still being mined but except for prospecting, most metallic mineral exploitation has ceased. A significant copper-molybdenum prospect has been found downstream from the confluence of Livengood Creek and the Tolovana River. Various claims have been staked in the Brooks and Alaska ranges, and intense prospecting is continuing. A large uranium deposit has been identified near the Charley River on Mount Prindle. Significant reserves of mercury,

antimony, nickel, and copper remain in the Fairbanks District, with other minerals, and may prove exploitable as access improves and ore prices increase. The overall mineral wealth of the Interior is hard to calculate because of production costs, location of the resource and shipping difficulties. Good quantities of some metallic minerals have been found, but the feasibility of exploiting them is in doubt.

Gigantic reserves of coal have also been identified. Estimated reserves of strippable coal consist of two billion tons of bituminous coal and five billion tons of subbituminous coal, with an inferred reserve of 120 billion tons. Deposits have been found near Rampart, Chicken, Hess Creek and on the Nation River. Fairly extensive deposits have also been identified near Eagle and Jarvis Creek, near Delta. The Jarvis Creek field is estimated to total 76 million tons of coal.

The Nenana coal field extends 80 miles along the north slope of the Alaska Range from Wood River to Kantishna River, with strippable coal reserves approaching 500 million tons. The only coal mine pres-

Opposite
Gold—the dream that brought the Outsiders to the Interior, to the Fortymile, to Birch Creek, to Fairbanks. And relics of these early searches are scattered throughout the Interior. This abandoned dredge rests in a pond near Fox, 11 miles north of Fairbanks and the junction of the Steese and Elliott Highways. (Ed Cooper)

Below
Miners at Usibelli Coal Mine on the Healy River see that operations at the chute proceed smoothly. (Mark Kelley)

Alaska National Interest Lands in the Interior

Passage of the Statehood Act and Alaska Native Claims Settlement Act provided for the distribution of federal land to federal and state governments and to the Native corporations. The U.S. Congress had several years to review Alaska's land resources and designate national monuments, parks, wildlife refuges, forests, and wild and scenic rivers. The bill passed by the House of Representatives in 1978 to resolve the issue was killed in the Senate. Consequently, to protect the land, the President and Secretary of the Interior, relying on powers vested in the executive branch, in separate actions, set aside 56 million acres as national monuments and 54 million acres as withdrawals under the Federal Land Policy Management Act.

In the Interior the lands set aside include northern and western extensions of Mount McKinley National Park. The new areas, plus an extension to the south not in the Interior region, are known as Denali National Monument. The purpose of this monument is to provide territory for outdoor activities that are minimally disruptive of the environment, such as hiking and backpacking; preservation of key wildlife habitat; and maintenance of the integrity of caribou migration routes.

Abutting the Canadian border is Yukon-Charley National Monument that protects a portion of the upper Yukon River with its historic, biotic and geologic resources and the Charles River drainage, a basically undisturbed wilderness watershed.

Efforts to maintain crucial waterfowl, raptor and mammal habitat have prompted the creation of Yukon Flats National Monument. In between Yukon-Charley and Yukon Flats is a stretch of Birch Creek that has been proposed as a wild and scenic river. And to the south of Yukon-Charley portions of the Fortymile River also have been proposed as a wild and scenic river.

In the central Brooks Range along the northern border of the Interior is the Gates of the Arctic National Monument—a wonderland for outdoor enthusiasts with good fishing, rafting, kayaking, canoeing, and suitable habitat for bears, wolves, wolverines, Dall sheep, moose, caribou, raptors and migrating birds.

In addition, there are five proposed national wildlife refuges: Kanuti, Koyukuk, Nowitna, a portion of the Innoko and, in the far southeastern corner of the region, the proposed Tetlin National Wildlife Refuge. Also proposed is an addition to the existing Arctic National Wildlife Range. The purpose of these refuges is to ensure adequate habitat for the survival of wildlife species. ☐

ently operating commercially in Alaska is Usibelli Coal Mine on the Healy River (please see page 100). Usibelli provides roughly 700,000 tons of coal per year and has produced almost 17 million tons of high-quality coal since 1918. The mine output is sold to the military, consumers in the Fairbanks area and the Golden Valley Electric Association plant at Healy, which transmits power to Fairbanks.

Petroleum exploration has been conducted throughout the region and several promising areas have been identified. The southern Brooks Range petroleum province is described as having moderate petroleum potential, while the Yukon Flats has a high rating for hydrocarbon fuels. The Kandik province is designated as having high potential, but test wells drilled on the Kandik River have all been dry. The middle Tanana and Minchumina basins have low petroleum potential, and a test hole drilled south of Nenana by Union Oil was also dry. The trans-Alaska oil pipeline traverses the Interior and was built to strict environmental standards which considered the region's unique geographic features.

୶

As in other areas of the state, clashes have occurred between resource developers and those interested in preserving the Interior's wild-land values. Some areas of high scenic and wilderness value also have high mineral values, and many lands in contention are within proposed national monuments and national wildlife refuges—all bound up in congressional debate over the D-2 lands issue as this edition went to press.
—*Tom Walker*

History: From Bark Canoes to Gas Pipelines

Ivan, a Tanana *tyone* or chief of Nuklakayet. (Lieutenant Allen's *Reconnaissance in Alaska*, written following his 1835 expedition and reprinted from *The ALASKA JOURNAL®*)

*I*n the minds of many people, the Great Interior did not exist until gold was discovered at Circle and Rampart and then Fairbanks at the turn of the century.

Just as no success occurs overnight, neither did the discovery of the Interior and its riches spring immediately into the limelight. This emergence took many years and the toil of explorers, exploiters, adventurers and prospectors who plied the waters and tramped the trails the Indians had trod many a century before them.

Even the Russian occupation of Alaska offered little change for the Interior tribes who lived as they always lived on the rivers and tributaries, sustaining themselves on salmon speared or netted. They dressed in buckskin made from moose and caribou killed by copper-tipped arrows; they lived in shelters of bark and brush. They were gatherers of berries, makers of bark canoes; they lived in an inhospitable land and they survived. The men were hunters; the women were clothes makers. In physical appearance the Athabascans are taller than Eskimos and not as stocky; they are swarthy, with high cheekbones, piercing black eyes and black hair.

The Athabascans of the Yukon basin, who numbered 7,000 in 1880, were a nonviolent people. When the stampede to the Interior began in the 1800's, the Athabascans adjusted, relocated and without question saved the lives of many white men who came unprepared into the vast Interior.

Father Julius Jette, camera in hand, with some of his friends on Nulato's main street, about 1904.
(Crosby Library, Gonzaga University; reprinted from *The ALASKA JOURNAL®*)

When the ill-equipped expedition of Army Lieutenant Joseph Castner ran out of provisions on the Tanana River in 1899, the men suffered exposure and hunger. Their clothes were in shreds and, in desperation, they ate their mules. Castner reported:

"... *it is but justice to say a few words for these friends of mine, who found us all but dead in the wilderness, with the Alaskan winter closing in around us. Entire strangers of another race, they received us as no friend of mine, white or colored, did before or since. They asked no questions and required no credentials. They were men. It was enough that their fellow beings were starving. Unknown to them were the wrongs our race had done theirs for centuries.*"

While the coastal villages of Alaska were frequently visited, the Interior remained little known to the white man until 1865 when Western Union began to survey for a telegraph line across Alaska to the Bering Strait. This line was to connect with the trans-Siberian line for telegraphic communications between America and Europe. Robert Kennicott, a naturalist who had been to Alaska on an earlier expedition, was in charge of the Alaska surveyors and the wire-stringing crew with orders to push ahead as fast as possible to complete the line before Cyrus Field laid his undersea cable across the Atlantic Ocean to England. The race was on.

The original fort at Fort Yukon was founded in 1847 as a Hudson's Bay trading post, about two miles from the present town of Fort Yukon. (Kathy Kollodge)

Among Kennicott's crew was a young scientist whose name ever after would be linked with Alaska—the naturalist William Dall. In August of 1865 Kennicott and his men reached Saint Michael near the mouth of the Yukon. At that point the party split into different groups and during the next two years several things happened: Kennicott died and Dall, at the age of 20, became leader of the scientific corps of the crew; the United States purchased Alaska from Russia; and Cyrus Field's sixth attempt to lay the trans-Atlantic cable succeeded. The Alaska telegraphic project was dead.

In all, Western Union had strung 80 miles of wire, but, more than that, the expedition had produced the first map of the entire 1,875-mile Yukon River, as well as scientific data in a dozen specialized areas including geology, anthropology, botany and zoology.

"The Interior everywhere needs exploration," Dall wrote, but no one was in any hurry to do it.

Two years later, in 1869, Captain Charles Raymond of the Corps of Engineers determined that the Hudson's Bay Company's trading post called Fort Yukon was well within Alaska's borders. With little persuasion necessary, the Canadians folded their tents and went home. Raymond's mission was the Army's only act of exploration in Alaska for more than a decade. With the retreat of the Canadians, "not one white man was left on the great river; the native tribes assumed their original sway over the Yukon basin," according to Judge James Wickersham in *Old Yukon* (1938).

It was not long before the Alaska Commercial Company established trading posts along the Yukon to accommodate the fur traders. The trappers and the traders, soon followed by prospectors, entered the country by canoe or by raft—all forerunners of the great migration to come.

In spite of the fact that Congress was stingy in appropriating funds to explore the Yukon basin, the intrepid Lieutenant Frederick Schwatka did his own investigating while on an official mission to count the Native population in 1883 and to determine their attitude toward the white man. Schwatka took a party of six to the headwaters of the Yukon River. They started with a 40-foot raft at Lake Lindeman in Canada and four months later arrived at Saint Michael, near where the river flows into the Pacific Ocean. This totally navigable river in summer, and frozen highway in winter, was the obvious route for penetration into the Interior. Schwatka kindled enthusiastic interest in this part of the country with the publication of his book, *Along Alaska's Great River* (1898), based on his explorations.

It is difficult to comprehend that 100 years ago many of Alaska's rivers, mountains, passes and minerals were unknown, untouched, untapped and untrampled. On to this scene enters Lieutenant Henry Tureman Allen whose incredible journey of 1,500 miles cut a new trail into the Interior. He discovered the Suslota Pass in the Alaska Range, discovered minerals of great wealth and made the first complete map of three major river systems—the Copper, the Tanana and the Koyukuk. It was this period of data gathering, map making and trail blazing that provided the wedge which cracked open the Interior and paved the way for the discovery of gold. When gold was discovered, it brought not only the miners, but their families, and that was the beginning of settlement in the Interior. No area is truly rooted without the presence of homemakers and schoolhouse raisers and business stakers.

But that is getting ahead of our story. Next in line of the Interior dwellers came the missionaries. Long before the gold rush began the Anglican, Episcopal and Catholic priests set out in the wilderness to establish missions along the Yukon River. As early as 1862 the Church of England sent missionaries into the Fort Yukon area where Archdeacon Robert McDonald spent 50 years working with the Indians. Bishop William Bompas conducted services among the inhabitants in the same part of the country in 1869. The Catholic Church dispatched Bishop Charles Seghers to the Interior in 1872 and he was eventually followed by Father Crimont and Father Jette. Mission schools, hospitals and boarding schools were established where Native children were taught manual skills, gardening and farming.

These missionaries endured the incredible loneliness, the inescapably severe weather, and the personal privations that accompanied it, and they also had the nearly impossible job of communicating with the Athabascans who have at least 58 different language stocks and hundreds of dialects.

Tay Thomas in her book, *Cry in the Wilderness* (1967), said "missionaries were the first people to put the Indian (and Eskimo) dialects into written form, and once that was done, they had to teach the Natives to read their own language. As a result the Bible, hymnals, and prayerbooks were among the first to be translated into the Athabascan language."

Dog team missionary Hudson Stuck, Episcopal archdeacon of the Yukon, covered nearly 2,000 miles every year from about 1904 to 1920, serving the missions along his Interior route from Eagle to points north. He had a deep affection for the Natives, their customs and skills. Stuck, a versatile man, wrote five books about Alaska including *Ten Thousand Miles With a Dog Sled* (1914), and *The Ascent of Denali* (1921), in which he told of his successful climb of Mount McKinley's South Peak.

One of the first men to make the 350-mile trip from Valdez to Fairbanks was Episcopal Bishop Peter Trimble Rowe who camped in -60°F weather during the 18-day trip. Rowe was a builder of missions and hospitals, including one in Fairbanks in 1904, and he developed rapport with the incoming white settlers. The Bishop crossed the Chilkoot Trail in 1896, two years before the Klondike stampede.

We know that the Klondike is not and never was in Alaska but many people thought it was and, as a

It is difficult to comprehend that 100 years ago many of Alaska's rivers, mountains, passes and minerals were unknown, untouched, untapped and untrampled.

Right
Felix Pedro, born about 1858, died in St. Joseph's Hospital in Fairbanks in 1910. Pedro's find at Discovery Creek led to the gold rush to the Tanana Valley and the founding of Fairbanks. (Reprinted from *The ALASKA JOURNAL®*)

Opposite
The Fairbanks waterfront on the Chena slough about 1914. The town was past her first boom by this time but with many gold dredges working the area's waterways, the waterfront was a busy place. (Washington State Historical Society, courtesy of Dexter Bartlett)

result, the gold strike that shook the Klondike sent tremors into Alaska. In came the stampeders, those disappointed by their luck in the Dawson environs, seeking their fortune in the Interior. The trails they blazed from Circle to Fairbanks, from Valdez to Fairbanks, and from Fairbanks to Livengood, became the roads of the future. The gold rush pumped capital into the wilderness and created a great influx of people into the Interior. Five years after gold was discovered in the Tanana Valley, Fairbanks was the largest city in Alaska.

The gold was always there, of course, buried beneath the permafrost, but the Tanana Valley was off the beaten track, not easily accessible, and remote from supply centers. Few white settlers made their

way into the region until the beginning of the 20th century. One of the earliest recorded visits was by Lieutenant Allen and his party in the summer of 1885 on a map-making trip. Thirteen years later Alfred H. Brooks, later to become the dean of a long line of Alaska geologists, descended the Tanana River with a party from the U.S. Geological Survey. At that time Brooks found "colors" on the river bars and suggested that prospecting might be good. For explorations in Alaska, Brooks Range bears his name. Brooks, a great admirer of Lieutenant Allen said, "No man through his own individual efforts had added more to our knowledge of Alaska than Lieutenant Allen."

Through the years many gold rush towns in Alaska, Canada, California and Colorado have sprung into being with a boom and died with barely a sigh. Not Fairbanks. This one-time gold camp on the banks of the Chena River, where the first business was established by E.T. Barnette nearly 80 years ago, still thrives as the commercial center of the Interior.

In the beginning, 1901, there was only the wilderness and the river and millions of dollars' worth of gold. By a great coincidence, at the time Barnette was establishing his trading post, Italian immigrant and prospector Felix Pedro found gold in the hills nearby. Pedro spotted the smoke of the riverboat docked on the Chena and came down from the hills to replenish his pack. Sight of the miner, who was well respected by his peers, gave Barnette hope that his cache location might be a favorable one after all. He was not there by choice. Due to low water, the Captain of the *LaVelle Young* had refused to take Barnette any farther upriver. Like it or not, Barnette was settled there for the winter. Less than a year later, on July 22, Pedro staked Discovery Claim and the rush was on. Pedro's discovery started a gold mining industry that out-produced all other mining districts in Alaska.

Waves of stampeders surged into Fairbanks to find a town of wooden sidewalks and mud-clogged streets. The dwellings were half-tent, half-frame, others were crude log shelters, situated along the curve of the Chena River, which would soon be spanned by a

Above
The U.S. Army established Eagle City Camp in 1899 at Eagle on the Yukon River. The Fort Egbert post was built a year later and abandoned in 1911.
(Courtesy of R.N. De Armond)

Right
Early-day placer miners haul dirt to the sluice box, then pour water over the earth to flush out the dirt and leave the heavier gold trapped in the bottom of the box.
(Courtesy of R.N. De Armond)

40

wooden bridge to link them with the creek towns yet to be discovered—Dome, Vault, Little Eldorado, Olnes, Livengood, Golden City and Ester. With axes, shovels and gold pans, the weary miners of former stampedes came by the hundreds, and so the Interior was won.

Another man who played a part in the founding of Fairbanks was Judge James Wickersham, first judge of the Third Judicial District, whose foresight, as well as political knack, prompted him to request that Barnette name his cache after the judge's own friend, Senator Charles Fairbanks, who later became Vice President of the United States under Theodore Roosevelt. To repay the favor, Judge Wickersham designated Fairbanks as the legal center of the Tanana Mining District over the rival town of Chena. During his long and illustrious career in Alaska, Wickersham served intermittently as Alaska Delegate to Congress between 1909 and 1933, introduced the first Alaska Railroad bill, the first Alaska statehood bill and was the first man to attempt to climb Mount McKinley. Wickersham's book *Old Yukon* is still being used and widely quoted, and in it he describes his first view of Fairbanks: "A half dozen new squat log structures, a few tents, and an incoming stream of dog teams and gold seekers, a small clearing in the primeval forest— that was Fairbanks as I first saw it on April 9, 1903."

All the supplies for this new boom town were imported from Seattle, a 2,700-mile ocean voyage to Saint Michael and an additional 1,200-mile trip by sternwheeler to Fairbanks—a six-week trip under favorable conditions. As new gold strikes were made near Pedro Creek, the rush gathered momentum and soon the need for a rail service to the creek towns was realized. Within three years after gold discovery a 45-mile narrow-gauge railroad was launched with private financing. As it was from the beginning, and is today, Fairbanks was a service and supply center for the Interior.

From the start Fairbanks differed from other boom towns; it was not a fly-by-night operation. The miners, graduates of earlier stampedes to Juneau, the Klon-dike and Nome, were seasoned Alaskans. They loved the North and were ready to settle permanently. Fairbanks was placer mining territory which meant the gold was anywhere from 80 to 200 feet below the frozen ground. It did not come out willingly. Time, money, men and equipment were needed, and in the meantime a town had to be built. The families came and Fairbanks grew.

It was a frontier town, no doubt about that. Saloons outnumbered churches and gambling was wide open day and night. Yet, it was not wild in the Wild West sense of things. "There were no gun fights, as I do not suppose one man in 500 carried a gun," observed John Clark in the book *Sourdough Sagas* by Herbert Heller (1967). "There was no poverty, for the population consisted almost without exception of able-bodied men and women, and work was plentiful and

Judge James Wickersham, first judge of the Third Judicial District out of Fairbanks, was one of the most illustrious of the early pioneers in the Interior. (Alaska Historical Library, reprinted from *The ALASKA JOURNAL®*)

Like gold towns throughout much of Alaska, Cleary—or Cleary City, as it was often called—prospered and died in the span of a few years. At its height, 1904-1906, Cleary Creek was the largest gold producer in the Tanana Valley. The city supported a cigar shop, clothing and drug stores, bakeries, banks and saloons. It also boasted of two hospitals, dentists, the Grand Hotel in the largest log building in the area, an Arctic Brotherhood Hall, electricity, telephones, a sawmill and piped-in water. But by 1908 gold was hard to find in upper Cleary Creek and the majority of the shopkeepers and miners had moved down the creek to Chatanika. (University of Alaska Archives)

well paid." In those days, Fairbanks was a town without locks.

In less than five years after gold discovery, Fairbanks was modern in every way—there were electric lights, steam heat, a city sewer system, fire and police department, a federal jail, courthouse and post office, a public school, two hospitals, one library, three newspapers, a handful of banks and numerous bath houses. As the years went by there were added six barber shops, four blacksmith shops, three chicken ranches, ten cigar stores, seven clothing stores, two dairies, one dance hall, six dentists, 11 doctors, 31 attorneys, five drugstores, six dry-goods stores, five dressmakers' parlors, three greenhouses, 14 grocery stores, eight hardware stores, 12 hotels, four ice cream parlors, four jewelry stores, one laundry (steam), five laundries (hand); three meat markets, two turkish baths, two paint and wallpaper houses, 11

restaurants, 15 saloons, two photographic studios, one undertaking parlor, and so forth.

Of course there was another side of life in Fairbanks— a city of contrasts from the beginning— and that was the majority of people roughing it frontier style in squat, cramped log cabins situated on permafrost. Here the water was delivered to the front door in five-gallon cans and carried out the back door in slop buckets. There was electricity but only one outlet—lightbulbs were often carried from room to room on an extension cord. Out back was the little house with the half moon, and a few lucky residents had a seat with a caribou fur liner. Wood-burning Yukon stoves warmed the cabins, but on bitterly cold nights the bed sheets froze to the wall.

People came to Fairbanks by sternwheeler in summer and over the Valdez snow trail in winter. When the rivers froze over there was no more freight, and

Left
Circle, one of the early mining communities, about 1906. The town was established in 1887 when L.N. McQuesten located a trading post nearby, making Circle one of the very early American settlements in Interior Alaska. The town owes its name to the assumption made by early traders and prospectors that the town was on the Arctic Circle.
(Courtesy of R.N. De Armond)

Below
The fire department of Circle, or Circle City as it was known in the early days. When the alarm sounded, the wooden-wheeled wagon was hauled down the boardwalk, buckets filled with water splashing all the way.
(Courtesy of R.N. De Armond)

Left
The steamer *Schwatka* ties up at the one-year-old metropolis of Ruby on the Yukon River, June 26, 1912.
(Courtesy of R.N. De Armond)

little chance of leaving the country. There were the long, solitary and lonely days to be gotten through. "I think my mother felt the unspeakable isolation more than she would ever say," wrote Margaret Murie in *Two in the Far North*. It was 1911 and Margaret remembers, "She kept it locked away inside, while she went serenely about the task that was hers—adapting her very civilized self to creating a home and bringing up a family on this far frontier, with the man she loved."

When Fairbanks was having its heyday, it was struck by two blows in succession that would have been the undoing of any lesser community. In 1905 a flood destroyed many homes and businesses along the Chena River. The following year, on a hot summer day, the tinder-box town, built of dry lumber with sawdust insulation, caught fire. In 42 minutes nearly the entire business district was destroyed, although not one life was lost. Wet blankets on the eaves of the Northern Commercial Company store prevented it from burning, and hundreds of pounds of bacon thrown into the NC boilers gave the water pumps enough pressure to contain the fire. True to its

Above
Chena, on the north bank of the Tanana River, one mile west of the mouth of the Chena River and seven miles southwest of Fairbanks, was called Chena Junction because it was the southern terminus of the Tanana Valley Railroad. However, in 1903 the town was incorporated as Chena. A post office was established in the town in 1903 and discontinued in 1918. By 1920, as Fairbanks grew and Chena died away, the town had only 18 inhabitants.
(Courtesy of R.N. De Armond)

Right
The paddlewheeler *Louise* on the Yukon, pushing barges filled with supplies. Steamboats moved up and down the Yukon to Dawson in Yukon Territory, and made side trips on the Tanana and Chena to Fairbanks and other Interior ports.
(Courtesy R.N. De Armond)

Gold was discovered on July 24, 1914, on Livengood Creek
by N.R. Hudson and Jay Livengood. The village, 50 miles
northwest of Fairbanks, was founded near their claim
as a mining camp during the winter of 1914-1915 when
hundreds of people came into the district. The post office
established there in 1915 was abandoned in 1957.
(Courtesy of R.N. De Armond)

. . . the history of the Interior repeats itself— adversity and triumph, threat and rescue . . .

Top
A pump moves water over the riffles of a sluice box along the Fortymile River. Over the past few years an average of approximately $15 million in cash flow has been generated from small mine production of gold, and other minerals.
(Harold Schetzle, reprinted from *ALASKA®* magazine)

Above
Chatanika, named for the Chatanika River and located about 20 miles northeast of Fairbanks, was founded about 1904 as a mining settlement. Visitors to the Fairbanks area can drive north along the Steese Highway to view one of the old gold dredges.
(Afton Blanc)

Below
Jet service is available in the Interior. Major airlines serve Fairbanks and Wien Air Alaska serves many of the smaller communities, such as Galena, where this Wien cargo jet is about to take off.
(Matthew Donohoe)

Right
The Alaska Railroad, operated by the Federal Railroad Administration of the U.S. Department of Transportation, provides passenger and freight service between Anchorage and Fairbanks. Here one of the trains passes through the Nenana Canyon near Usibelli.
(Tom Walker)

pioneering spirit, Fairbanks did not give up—even before the ashes cooled, the sound of the carpenter's hammer was heard in the land.

From the beginning that has been the story of Fairbanks—adversity and triumph, threat and rescue. Gold mining petered out in 1910 and the future looked grim, but the Alaska Railroad bill was passed by Congress and the building of the line from Seward to the Fairbanks terminus revived the local economy and made accessible the much-needed fuel supply of the Healy coal mines. This was followed by the founding of the Alaska Agricultural College and School of Mines, which opened in Fairbanks in 1922 with six students and an equal number of faculty. That institution became the University of Alaska, which today is one of the major sources of income in Fairbanks, along with military expenditures and the tourist industry.

In 1927 the Fairbanks Exploration Company, a subsidiary of the U.S. Mining, Refining and Smelting Company, began gold-dredging operations that employed almost every able-bodied man in town. At the same time, airplanes were introduced in the Interior. Since then the sky has been the limit in aviation development. Mail flights to the bush originated in Fairbanks, and soon scheduled flights linked the Interior with Southwestern Alaska. In 1940 Pan American Airways began scheduled service between Fairbanks and Seattle. Today jumbo jets make several flights daily to Fairbanks. With the North Pole refinery nearby, Fairbanks has captured the refueling trade of the Japanese and Korean Airlines. The refinery has a capacity of more than 30,000 barrels of crude oil per day.

The strategic military importance of the Interior was realized on the eve of World War II when the Army Corps of Engineers began building the 1,500-mile Alaska Highway between Alaska, Canada and the Lower 48. The record-breaking road construction feat was started in 1942 and completed the following year. (It was open to public traffic in 1948.) During the war Fairbanks was the site of the Air Corps test station, named Ladd Field (now Fort Wainwright), which

One of the Interior's major industrial complexes is the oil refinery at North Pole, just outside Fairbanks. The facility has a capacity of more than 30,000 barrels of crude oil per day and it is the availability of this oil that enabled Fairbanks to garner the refueling trade of the Japanese and Korean airlines.
(Ron Dalby)

became the transfer point for "lend-lease" military planes for Russia. American pilots brought the planes to Ladd, and Russian pilots flew them across Alaska to Siberia and the eastern front.

Alaska historian William Hunt in his book *Alaska: A Bicentennial History* (1976), wrote, "World War II brought to Alaska the biggest boom the territory had experienced, bigger than any of the gold rushes of the past." At that time the federal government pumped more than $1 billion into Alaska.

After the war both Ladd Field and Eielson Air Force Base, 30 miles from Fairbanks, became permanent facilities. As the mining activity decreased, the military expenditures increased with Fairbanks as the launching pad for the DEW Line (distant early warning system) and White Alice as the nation's radar posts for defense against a transarctic attack.

Before statehood, Fairbanks was the site of the Constitutional Convention held on campus of the University of Alaska in 1955, and four years later statehood was granted. Statehood did not mean an immediate end to problems. By 1967 the Fairbanks economy was once again in trouble and unemployment was high. That fall the Chena River, after a

week of unprecedented rainfall, rose 18 feet above its normal level, inundating the city and driving thousands of people from their homes. The flood caused $200 million in damages and the city became a national disaster area. With typical fighting spirit (and the aid of federal money) Fairbanksans rebuilt. One year later Fairbanks was named an All-American City.

Meantime, a vast reserve of oil was discovered at Prudhoe Bay, 400 miles north, and Fairbanks became the logistics headquarters for the oil operation. Alyeska Pipeline Service Company, builder of the trans-Alaska pipeline, and its affiliated contractors, spent $1 million a day for two years in Fairbanks. That was the economic transfusion the city needed, and, as always, it came in the nick of time. In less than two years the community of 40,000 swelled to a population of 65,000.

The Fairbanks airport went from a deficit operation to the most active airport in the state for freight as the huge airlift got under way. Nearly 100 companies in the oil industry—and related businesses—set up offices in Fairbanks, resulting in a housing shortage, traffic congestion, crowded schools and overtaxed

The trans-Alaska pipeline, an 800-mile monument to private enterprise, carries oil from the Prudhoe Bay oil fields on the North Slope to the terminal port at Valdez on Prince William Sound. Here the pipeline crosses the Tanana River near Fairbanks. (Art Wolfe)

services, as well as an increase in crime. At the height of the pipeline construction, 22,000 people were working at the camps. The oil rush brought more people, more money and more problems than any other boom in the history of the Interior.

Construction of the pipeline—which cost $8 billion, the most expensive project undertaken by private industry—was started in 1973. The parallel North Slope Haul Road from Fairbanks to Prudhoe Bay took five months to build, with ownership reverting to the state after the pipeline was completed. Future development of Fairbanks could hinge in part on the state's willingness to maintain the road and make it available for public use.

Today Fairbanks awaits the next major construction phase—the building of a natural gas pipeline from the North Slope to the Lower 48 via Fairbanks and the Alaska Highway. It is a new peak to conquer, and the history of the Interior repeats itself— adversity and triumph, threat and rescue, with each boom period leveling off at a new, higher plateau. Since the first shovelful of Pedro paydirt, people have been coming to this land between the ranges, where there is room enough to expand for generations to come.

—*Jo Anne Wold*

49

Along the Rivers

*M*ost visitors to Interior Alaska see only a small corner of the country— that portion touched by the state's limited highway system . . . Fairbanks, Mount McKinley National Park and perhaps a few communities along the Taylor, Steese or Elliott highways.

The "other" Interior is connected by a far more elaborate transportation network—the river highways that for centuries have connected people and villages of the vast Yukon River drainage.

Rivers are the heart of life in these villages, providing transportation throughout the year (by boats in the summer and snow machines or dog sleds in the winter), and bringing food to people in the form of salmon and a variety of fresh-water fish.

There are more than three dozen major villages strung out along the rivers of the Interior, mainly on the Yukon, Tanana and Koyukuk. A few Interior villages also are found on the upper Kuskokwim, a waterway that is far more crowded farther downstream in Eskimo country.

In the following section we'll look at the villages of the Interior, starting at the Alaska-Yukon Territory border and drifting generally downriver . . . with a few side trips along the way.

Breakup along the Yukon River usually means a brief season of flooding for many riverfront villages. This photo was taken in early May downriver from Fort Yukon. The ice was three to four feet thick and moving at about six miles per hour. (Dennis and Debbie Miller)

Yukon River

*A*wesome in size, the historic Yukon River today continues as a focal point of life in the Interior—as a source of food for many river villages, and a watery highway for travel and trade through lowlands of the Interior.

The Yukon is easily the longest river in Alaska, wandering 1,400 miles through the state from the Alaska-Yukon border to the Bering Sea coast. Farther upstream, between the border and its headwaters, is another 475 miles of river.

Actual headwaters are in Marsh Lake, Yukon Territory, southeast of Whitehorse.

While the Yukon River is associated strongly with gold rushes of the late 1800's—as an access route to the Klondike and other prospecting hot spots of the day—the river had been well-known to Natives for centuries. Eskimos of the lower Yukon descriptively called the river *Kuikpak,* meaning "big river." Interior Athabascans gave the river its present name, which probably also meant "big river."

The upper Yukon region within Alaska includes the Porcupine and other major Interior tributaries, the Chandalar, Tanana (and its tributary, the Nenana) and Koyukuk.

Left
A view of the Yukon River near Eagle, not far from the Alaska-Yukon Territory border.
(Chris Stall, Stone Flower Studio)

Right
Calico Cliffs, striated rock formations, are found along the Yukon River not far from Eagle. This portion of the river is near the boundary of the Yukon-Charley National Monument.
(Nancy Simmerman)

Strips of salmon hang on a drying rack along the Yukon River in July, near the height of the annual river fishery.
(Nancy Simmerman)

FORTYMILE COUNTRY

The Fortymile region, south of Eagle near the Alaska-Yukon Territory border, was the scene of a prospecting rush that began in 1886 with the discovery of gold near the Fortymile River. The settlement of Fortymile, now a ghost town, *(right)* was established in 1903 as a U.S. Army Signal Corps telegraph station—originally called North Fork because it was at the junction of Bullion Creek and the North Fork of the Fortymile River.
(George Wuerthner)

Below
There's still gold to be found, as a Fortymile River prospector demonstrates. This collection of nuggets resulted from a dredging-and-panning operation along the river, not far from the site of the first gold discoveries in 1886.
(Harold Schetzle)

EAGLE

Right
Eagle (population 200), six miles west of the Alaska-Yukon Territory border along the Yukon River, was established as Belle Isle by Moses Mercier in 1874, and operated now and then until its development as a mining camp in 1898. The village, by then boasting a population of about 800, was platted and named Eagle City for the bald eagles that nested on nearby Eagle Bluff—seen in the background here. The U.S. Army moved to Eagle in 1899 to establish a camp, and the following year built Fort Egbert, which was abandoned by 1911. The village is at the end of the Taylor Highway, 161 miles northeast of Tetlin Junction on the Alaska Highway. Interest in the settlement has increased in recent years, and Eagle today has a few stores, two gas stations, a restaurant, cabins and a roadhouse with meals and lodging. The village has scheduled air service from Fairbanks and Tok and charter services based in Eagle. In recent years townspeople and the Bureau of Land Management have been restoring historic buildings in the area, including what's left of Fort Egbert.
(Gil Mull)

Above
Old buildings at Eagle include the first city hall, at right, built in 1901. Eagle was the trading center for miners and prospectors who objected to Canadian laws and taxes in the nearby Klondike area of Yukon Territory. During the gold rush many claims were staked in the Eagle area and town lots sold for as much as $1,000.
(Chris Stall, Stone Flower Studio)

Right
A fisherman picks a large king salmon from his set net along the Yukon River, near Eagle. The fish, on its spawning run upriver in July, has started turning color.
(Nancy Simmerman)

55

WOODCHOPPER AND COAL CREEKS

Below
An old gold dredge at Coal Creek near the Yukon River between Circle and Eagle. The earliest recorded claim at Coal Creek was in 1912 but men were mining the creek long before then. Between 1934 and 1954 a company owned by Ernest Patty—later president of the University of Alaska—recovered an estimated $4 million in gold from Coal Creek. The creek has been mined in recent years by AU Placer, Inc., although its future has been in some doubt since falling within the boundaries of the Yukon-Charley National Monument administered by the National Park Service.
(Gil Mull)

Right
The riverboat *Brainstorm II* pushes a supply barge up the Yukon River near Woodchopper Creek, between Circle and Eagle. Riverboats have served settlements along the Yukon for the past 80 years, but it's been 20 years since the last large steam paddlewheeler was retired from regular service.
(Gil Mull)

56

CIRCLE

Above
Circle (population 76), 50 miles south of the Arctic Circle along the banks of the Yukon River, is at the end of the Steese Highway—162 miles northeast of Fairbanks. The settlement is the northernmost point in Alaska to which it's possible to drive from the interconnecting public highway system of the United States and Canada. (Travelers can now drive farther north on the Dempster Highway, which passes through Yukon Territory on its way to Inuvik, Northwest Territories. And the trans-Alaska pipeline haul road winds farther north, but is not open to the public.) Circle was established in 1887 when L.N. McQuesten built a trading post nearby, making Circle one of the earliest American settlements in the Interior.
(Gil Mull)

Upper right
Meandering branches of Birch Creek, photographed near Circle in late summer. Many rivers and streams wander indecisively through the rolling Interior country, often forming horseshoe lakes (such as the lake in the upper right corner of the photo) as they seek new channels.
(Gil Mull)

Right
Sunset at Circle, December 29 at 2 P.M. On the shortest day of the year (a week before this photo was taken) the sun appears for only a few hours at Circle and other villages of the northern Interior.
(Gil Mull)

Fort Yukon, photographed May 5, 1979, as ice
on the Yukon River breaks up in the background.
(Dennis and Debbie Miller)

FORT YUKON
AND YUKON FLATS

Fort Yukon (population 700), commercial hub of the Yukon Flats area, is situated a short distance upstream from the confluence of the Porcupine and Yukon rivers and about eight miles north of the Arctic Circle. It is here that the Yukon begins its great bend, turning from a northwesterly course to a southwesterly flow toward the Bering Sea.

Fort Yukon was founded in 1847 by Alexander Hunter Murray of the Hudson's Bay Company—the actual site of the first trading post being about two miles downstream from the present town. Fort Yukon marked one of the extreme western penetrations of the HBC, since it took almost three years for trading goods to leave England, be carried across Canada by York boat and canoes to the Mackenzie River Delta, then be transported over the Richardson Mountains and down the Bell and Porcupine rivers to the post.

Right
Sled dogs await the winter season in their doghouse neighborhood behind a general store in Fort Yukon.
(Charlotte Casey, Staff)

The Yukon Flats, the lowland area on both sides of the Yukon River where it ceases its northward movement and bends to the west, is a paradise for wildlife. More than 130 species of birds, many of them migratory, have been identified in the area. Thirteen species, particularly grouse and songbirds, are residents in the flats. From 10% to 15% of the continental breeding population of canvasback ducks are mingled with mallards, pintails, American widgeons, northern shovelers, lesser Canada geese and white-fronted geese. There are a few families of rare trumpeter swans in the area as well as three species of loons and twelve species of shorebirds. Add to this a grebe population in excess of 100,000. More than 10,000 sandhill cranes use the area in the summer and several species of raptors feed on the abundant smaller birds and mammals. Both bald and golden eagles share the skies with ospreys, red-tailed hawks, gyrfalcons and the endangered American race of the peregrine falcons.

Mammals make good use of the flats as well. More than 850 Dall sheep have been counted in the White Mountains and Tanana Hills bordering the flats. Two caribou herds, the Porcupine and the Fortymile, graze in the area. Over 5,000 moose winter here and the entire Yukon Flats ecosystem supports populations of brown/grizzly and black bears, wolves, and many species of fur bearers including beavers, muskrats, mink, and marten, lynx, red foxes and coyotes.

Left
Its smaller size and more pointed muzzle distinguish the coyote from the other wild member of the canine family that occurs in Yukon Flats, the wolf.
(Stephen Krasemann)

Left
Three races of peregrine falcons, the arctic, American and Peale's, occur in Alaska and two of them, the Arctic and American, are severely endangered. The Yukon Flats, where it nests along the river cliffs and relies on swift flight to overtake smaller birds and mammals, is one of the last footholds of the American race.
(Myron Wright)

Above
A few families of the rare trumpeter, North America's largest swan, occur in the flats.
(Tom Walker)

Right
The elegant pintail is just one of 130 species of birds which use the Yukon Flats for a nesting or staging area.
(Penny Rennick, Staff)

61

Porcupine River

Right
The Porcupine River originates in northern Yukon Territory and flows southwestward to the Yukon River, joining the Yukon two miles northwest of the town of Fort Yukon. The western portion of the Porcupine is within the boundaries of the Yukon Flats National Monument.
(Reprinted from *ALASKA GEOGRAPHIC®*)

CHALKYITSIK

Below
Chalkyitsik, a small village on the Black River, which joins the Porcupine River 17 miles northeast of Fort Yukon in the Yukon Flats region, has an Athabascan name reported to mean "to fish with a hook, at the mouth of the creek." Other earlier names for the village included Fishhook, Fishhook Town and Fishhook Village.
(Bartz Englishoe)

Chandalar River

The Chandalar River flows 100 miles from the south slopes of the Brooks Range to the Yukon River 20 miles northwest of Fort Yukon. Arctic Village is along the East Fork of the Chandalar, and Venetie is near the main river not far from its confluence with the Yukon . . . otherwise the Chandalar drainage is almost uninhabited.

VENETIE

Left
The village of Venetie (population 148), near the Chandalar River northwest of Fort Yukon. This photo was taken during breakup of the rivers in early May.
(Dennis and Debbie Miller)

ARCTIC VILLAGE

Left
Arctic Village (population 111), northernmost major settlement in the Interior, is on the East Fork of the Chandalar River in the Brooks Range, 110 miles north of the Arctic Circle and 235 miles northeast of Fairbanks. This photo was taken at 9:30 P.M., May 13, just as breakup was occurring along rivers of the region.
(Dennis and Debbie Miller)

Below
Timothy Pike, left, of Arctic Village cooks a fillet of fish the traditional way—on a willow branch over an open fire.
(Dennis and Debbie Miller)

BEAVER

Right
The Athabascan village of Beaver, 60 miles southwest of Fort Yukon on the Yukon River. It was established as a river landing in 1906 and became a supply point for nearby gold diggings in 1911—but only briefly. This view was in May, during breakup of the river. (Dennis and Debbie Miller)

Below
The post office and store at Beaver (population 83). (Bartz Englishoe)

Francis Henry of Beaver tries out a new Troy tiller in a long-neglected garden—part of a program to encourage agricultural development in Athabascan villages. The project is sponsored by the Tanana Chiefs Conference. (Bartz Englishoe)

PURGATORY

Right
Purgatory, along the Yukon River 20 miles southwest of Beaver, was the home of Bill and Herman Yanert for about 40 years—from 1903, when Bill built the first cabin until the early 1940's when Herman left after his brother's death. The brothers fished, hunted, trapped and raised vegetables, and Bill wrote and illustrated hundreds of copies of *Yukon Breezes*, a poetry-and-paintings book he sold to river travelers for $5 per copy. This watercolor of their place at Purgatory, including a totem carved by Bill and Herman, was accompanied by the following poem: "There are cities famed in song and story / And some are not that ought to be / And such a place is Purgatory / Where the world's turmoil you never see!" (Reprinted from *The ALASKA JOURNAL®*)

STEVENS VILLAGE

Left
According to local sources, Stevens Village (population 78), on the Yukon River 54 miles downstream from Beaver, was founded by three brothers from Kokrines—Old Jacob, Gochonayeeya and Old Steven. The village was first called Denyeet, meaning "canyon," but when Old Steven was elected chief in 1902 the village took its present name. This may be the same Athabascan village referred to as Shamansville by survey parties in 1898.
(Tom Walker)

RAMPART

Lower left
An aerial view of Rampart (population 58), located on the south bank of the Yukon River, 61 miles up from Tanana. Rampart is a small Athabascan village with a colorful past. When gold was discovered in the nearby Minook Creek drainage in 1896, Rampart City became the principal supply point for the ensuing rush. The town was said to have a population of about 1,500 during its best days of 1898 and 1899, but by the turn of the century, the number of residents had dwindled. Rampart faced extinction in the early 1960's when the U.S. Corps of Engineers discussed plans for a huge hydroelectric dam in the Rampart Gorge area—a dam which would have flooded a large portion of the Yukon Flats area. This view of Rampart was taken in April when the Yukon was still frozen over.
(Nancy Simmerman)

Tanana River

The Tanana flows 531 miles northwest from Northway Junction (at the confluence of the Chisana and Nabesna rivers) to the Yukon River a few miles east of the village of Tanana.

An important river in terms of navigation and trade—especially between Nenana and its meeting with the Yukon River—the Tanana was once known by Indians as "mountain river," or "River of the Mountain Men," perhaps because it flows along the north flank of the Alaska Range from its headwaters area to about Delta Junction.

TANANA

Upper right
The waterfront at Tanana, an Athabascan settlement at the confluence of the Yukon and Tanana rivers—a long-established trading locality. The village of about 500 is the site of Nuchalawoyya, a summer festival which brings together Athabascan people from towns and villages throughout the Interior.
(Alissa Crandall)

Right
Tod Kozevnikoff, an Athabascan fisherman from Tanana, pulls king salmon from his set net.
(Len Sherwin)

Below
Fifty-pound buckets of salmon roe are prepared for packaging in Tanana. The salmon eggs are sold as a delicacy in the Orient.
(Len Sherwin)

MINTO

Youngsters paddle a canoe near the village of Minto (population 199), which in 1971 moved from the banks of the Tanana River up the Tolovana River to a point 11 miles from the Elliott Highway—and connected to the Elliott by road.
(Alissa Crandall)

NENANA

Nenana is a real crossroads town—at the junction of the Nenana and Tanana rivers, and situated along both the George Parks Highway and tracks of the Alaska Railroad.

Forty-five miles southwest of Fairbanks, Nenana is one of the main river-freight centers in Alaska and boat traffic always is heavy in the summer months.

The town (population 508) was first known as the Tortella area—a white man's interpretation of the Athabascan word *Toghotthele.* In 1902 Jim Duke built a post in Nenana where he traded with nomadic Athabascans and supplied goods and lodging for all river travelers.

The settlement grew rapidly during construction of the Alaska Railroad and on the day of completion—July 5, 1923—President Warren G. Harding drove a golden spike commemorating the event on the north side of rail bridge across the Tanana River.

Nenana has several other activities including a full schedule of dog sled races, snowmobile races, potlatches and the Yukon 800, an outboard-riverboat race.

Upper left
The George Parks Highway bridge crosses the Tanana River in the foreground, with the Alaska Railroad span farther upriver. The Nenana River comes into the Tanana at lower right. This photo was taken in April, not long before breakup of the Tanana River ice.
(Ron Dalby)

Left
Nenana is well known for the annual Nenana Ice Classic (legal for residents of Alaska only), which usually offers $100,000 in cash prizes to lucky winners who can guess the exact minute of the Tanana River ice breakup . . . always in April or May. The Nenana Ice Classic building is connected by wires to a tripod anchored in Tanana River ice.

The classic began in 1917 with a purse of $800, and has become an exciting community event. Ice pool speculation reaches a feverish pitch just before breakup time, as residents turn out in large numbers to help count and sort the thousands of tickets. The work of registering tickets goes on day and night until the task is completed. This photo was taken in May, shortly before breakup.
(Tom Walker)

Nenana River

The Nenana, with headwaters at Nenana Glacier in the Alaska Range, flows north 140 miles to the Tanana River at the town of Nenana.

Originally named *Tutlut* by Athabascans in the region, the Nenana was later dubbed Cantwell River by Lieutenant Henry Allen in 1885 for a lieutenant in the Revenue Cutter Service.

The river today is a popular spot for white-water adventurers who plunge through its canyons in rafts and kayaks, especially in the Mount McKinley National Park entrance area. (The river parallels the George Parks Highway between McKinley Park and Rex, affording many put-in and take-out sites for boats.)

RUBY

Left
Ruby (population 220), about 100 air miles downstream from Tanana on the Yukon River, was a booming town of more than 1,000 during early gold rushes along the Yukon. Gold was discovered on Ruby Creek near the site of the village in 1907, and on Long Creek in 1911. A stampede followed the second discovery and a substantial town developed within one year.
(Chris Stall, Stone Flower Studio)

Above
A modest sawmill operation at Ruby. Note the similar sawmill in a 1912 photograph of Ruby on page 43.
(Alissa Crandall)

Right
A view of Ruby, including an old wind generator on the left.
(Charlotte Casey, Staff)

GALENA

Above
Galena (population 631), 270 miles due west of Fairbanks on the Yukon River, has a large airfield (in the background of this photo). Before becoming a supply point for galena (lead ore) prospects in 1919, the village was called Natulaten.
(Chris Stall, Stone Flower Studio)

Below
Robert Attla of Galena nails together a frame for his new riverboat. Flat-bottom, shallow-draft skiffs are common along the length of the Yukon and other Interior rivers.
(Betsy Hart)

69

KOYUKUK

Shown here in December, the village of Koyukuk (population 109),is on the Yukon River 30 miles west of Galena. The village is near a noticeable bend in the Yukon, where the river turns from a westerly course to a southwesterly flow toward the Bering Sea—deflected abruptly by the Nulato Hills behind Koyukuk.
(Matthew Donohoe)

Below
A sign of the times at Koyukuk. Debby Pitka has just given her youngster a bath with help from the village's new safe-water plant. Fresh-water plants have been planned for most all villages in the Interior, with help from government funds.
(Matthew Donohoe)

Koyukuk River

The Koyukuk River, in the northwest portion of Alaska's Great Interior country, is 554 miles long, and flows southwest from the south slope of the Brooks Range to its meeting with the mighty Yukon River northeast of Nulato.

Villages in the Koyukuk drainage area include Allakaket, Alatna, Hughes, Huslia and Koyukuk—the latter near the confluence of the Yukon and Koyukuk rivers.

The Koyukuk has had more different names than most rivers in history. The first Koyukan Indian name recorded was Kukukak—or at least that is what Russian explorer L.A. Zagoskin called the river. Other names included Yunaka, Kuiuk, Kuyaak and Coyukuk.

Left
Rodger Dayton retrieves his water the traditional way. Dayton lives in Koyukuk and doesn't particularly like the taste of water from the safe-water plant so he cuts his own during winter. He first clears off snow from the area he's going to cut, then scribes block shapes with an ax. Dayton next breaks a hole in the ice to insert his saw and quickly cuts 100- to 150-pound blocks which are finally lugged to his cabin. The job completed, he can relax with a cup of coffee and look outside his window to see a winter's supply of drinking water stacked neatly in tiers.
(Matthew Donohoe)

HUSLIA

Left

Huslia (population 241), was settled in the late 1940's and early 1950's, on the banks of the Koyukuk River 70 miles north of Galena, when the Koyukan Athabascan population of a settlement called Cutoff moved to the new location four miles away. The name was changed to Huslia in 1952—the new name taken from a local stream.
(Lael Morgan, Staff, reprinted from *ALASKA*® magazine)

Below

Handicrafts, including Athabascan beadwork, are taught at art classes in Huslia.
(Matthew Donohoe)

HUGHES

Left

Hughes (population 100), 85 miles northwest of Tanana, is on the Koyukuk River midway between Allakaket and Huslia. The village was established in 1910 as a riverboat landing and port of supply for the nearby Indian River diggings, and was named for Charles Evans Hughes, then governor of New York. The town flourished for five years and after the gold ran out the settlement evolved into a Koyukan Athabascan village.
(Chris Stall, Stone Flower Studio)

Back-Country Boating

The Interior's rivers have been highways for Athabascan travelers for centuries, and in more recent years they have become a playground for visitors from other parts of Alaska . . . other parts of the world. Attention has been focused, in particular, on the Yukon River, traveled by many who wish to recreate gold rush voyages, and on the southern slopes of the Brooks Range, especially the Gates of the Arctic National Monument. As these photos show, river travelers are going at it in every imaginable way . . . □

Clockwise from left
► Rafters drift down the Alatna River, which flows through the heart of the Brooks Range to join the Koyukuk at Allakaket. The river is one of the state's most scenic, running through the Gates of the Arctic National Monument.
(John and Margaret Ibbotson)
► Some folks prefer the do-it-yourself method. These adventurers nailed together a simple raft with an improvised shelter and oil barrel stove, and floated down the Yukon in the style of early gold stampeders. They were photographed near Eagle, just west of the Alaska-Yukon Territory border.
(George Wuerthner)
► Brooks Range visitors rest after hauling an 18-foot aluminum canoe over a forested ridge from Takahula Lake to the Alatna River. From this point the boaters drifted 12 miles down the Alatna to Takahula River, then paddled and pulled the canoe up the Takahula until running out of water near Takahula Lake—the intended end of a triangular trip.
(Penny Rennick, Staff)
► A back-country traveler lines his kayak up the Charley River, an 88-mile-long tributary on the Yukon which joins the big river midway between Eagle and Circle in the Yukon-Charley National Monument.
(George Wuerthner)

ALATNA, ALLAKAKET

Right
Alatna, on the right bank, and Allakaket, on the left (combined populations 178), share the Koyukuk River near its junction with the Alatna River. The twin-villages concept was created shortly after the turn of the century by a missionary, Archdeacon Hudson Stuck, who wrote: "I was . . . impressed with the eligibility of that spot as a mission site. It was but 10 miles above the present Native village [Moses Village], and, with church and school established, the whole population would sooner or later move to it. Moreover, the Alatna River is the highway between the Kobuk and the Koyukuk . . . I foresaw two villages, one clustered about the church [Allakaket, an Athabascan village], the other lower down on the opposite side of the river [Alatna, Eskimo]. So I staked a mission site . . . almost opposite the mouth of the Alatna." Stuck later became well known for leading the first party to successfully climb the south peak of Mount McKinley.
(Chris Stall, Stone Flower Studio)

BETTLES FIELD

Above
Bettles Field, looking north to the Koyukuk River and foothills of the Brooks Range. Jumping-off point for Gates of the Arctic National Monument, Bettles Field has a lodge, trading post and Federal Aviation Administration facility at its busy airfield. The village has a population of about 88 and an extreme temperature range of -70°F (record set in 1975) to +92°F (reached in July 1955). Bettles Field and its suburb, Evansville, are 35 miles north of the Arctic Circle.
(Gil Mull)

Left
Bettles (often called Old Bettles), five miles downriver from Bettles Field was settled in 1899 when Gorden Bettles established a trading post along the Koyukuk River. Construction of an airport upriver in 1945 prompted a gradual migration to the new Bettles Field townsite.
(Gil Mull)

Top
Bettles Lodge offers food and several rooms to visitors, who include Brooks Range backpackers in the summer and hunters in the fall.
(John and Margaret Ibbotson)

Above
Fuel comes to bush villages in 55-gallon drums—the ubiquitous "tundra daisies" of the Arctic. These rows of drums were seen at Bettles Field, with Bettles Lodge in the background.
(Charlotte Casey, Staff)

WISEMAN

Below
Wiseman (summer population 18), saw an influx of strangers during construction of the trans-Alaska pipeline, which begins climbing toward Atigun Pass in the Wiseman area. The village is 60 miles north of the Arctic Circle on the middle fork of the Koyukuk River in the foothills of the Brooks Range.
(Gil Mull)

Right
This collapsing log building at Wiseman was Martin Slisco's roadhouse in earlier times. The village was settled in 1911 when the local population began to abandon Coldfoot, 10 miles to the south, in response to mining activity on Nolan and Wiseman creeks. The new town eventually took the name of the creek.
(Gil Mull)

75

NULATO

Right

The village of Nulato (population 365), is 35 miles west of Galena, one of the westernmost Athabascan villages in the Yukon River drainage. This photo shows the village in December, with a small amount of open water remaining in the Yukon at lower right. (Matthew Donohoe)

Below

Philip Madrose hauls water home by hand—to keep young, he says. It was wash day and he made several trips to the creek where a hole in the ice had been kept open in December. (Matthew Donohoe)

Kuskokwim River

*T*he Kuskokwim River, with tributaries flowing out of the north slope of the Alaska Range, near the southwest corner of Alaska's Interior, is one of the state's longest rivers.

Only the upper third of the river—small and somewhat unknown compared to the wide, sweeping lower river—remains within the boundaries we have defined for the Great Interior. Although the lower river is navigable by large tugs, barges and other vessels, only smaller outboard-driven skiffs and other shallow-draft boats can navigate the upper Interior portion.

McGRATH

McGrath (population 350), one of the only major Kuskokwim River settlements in the Interior, is 150 miles west of Mount McKinley between the Kuskokwim Mountains and the Alaska Range. A small trading post was established here in 1907 for the new diggings on the Innoko River, and the town which sprang up was named for a deputy marshall who established headquarters here the same year.
(Charlotte Casey, Staff)

Right
Employees of the Bureau of Land Management make music during a Fourth of July celebration at McGrath. The town has a number of government employees— notably BLM and the Federal Aviation Administration personnel.
(Alissa Crandall)

Along the Highways

*R*oads are crucial to the movement of people and goods in the Interior. Many of the state's highways are in the Interior and the Alaska Highway is perhaps the best known to Outsiders as the entry route to Alaska. Fairbanks serves as the transportation and service center for the Interior. The Interior's highway system includes the Elliott and Steese highways, the North Slope Haul Road, the Alaska Highway, the Taylor Highway and portions of the Richardson and George Parks Highways.

Opposite
The snowy peaks of the Alaska Range are visible to travelers southbound from Delta on the Richardson Highway.
(Tom Walker)

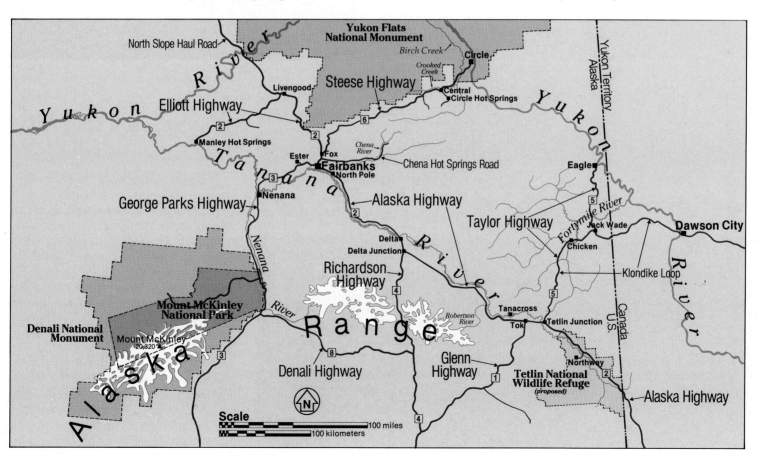

Clockwise from right

► In the 1920's American bison were transplanted to the Delta Junction area. The mammals thrived in their new home and the herd now numbers several hundred. Their penchant for grain has lead the farmers of the area to be less than enthusiastic about their big neighbors and attempts have been made to control the grazing and numbers of the herd. (Tom Walker)

► George Sickel tries his luck in the Robertson River, near the Alaska Highway, 16 miles northwest of Tanacross (population 128). The river was named in 1885 by Lieutenant Allen, an early explorer, for Sergeant Cady Robertson, a member of his exploration party. The river heads at the terminus of Robertson Glacier and flows northeast 33 miles to join the Tanana River. (John and Margaret Ibbotson)

► Thunderheads gather over the Alaska Highway between Northway (population 36), and Tok (population 735). The Alaska Highway descends for nearly 300 miles from the Alaska/Yukon border along the valley of the Tanana River to Fairbanks. (Gil Mull, reprinted from *ALASKA* magazine)

THE ALASKA HIGHWAY

Designed during World War II to relieve Alaska's reliance on shipping and to develop a land route to the north, the Alaska Highway (Alaska Route 2), which extends 1,500 miles from Dawson Creek, British Columbia to Fairbanks, was built by the U.S. Army Corps of Engineers under an agreement with the United States and Canada governments. The first contingent from the Corps of Engineers arrived at Dawson Creek, British Columbia, in March 1942. Crews worked north and south from Whitehorse, Yukon Territory, south from Delta Junction, Alaska, and north from Dawson Creek. Actual meeting of construction teams occurred in October 1942, but the highway was officially opened November 20, 1942.

THE RICHARDSON HIGHWAY

The Richardson (Alaska Route 4), was Alaska's first highway and follows the route of the Abercrombie and Richardson trails. The original route was a pack trail, for horses in summer and dog teams in winter. A route to Eagle, on the Yukon River, from Valdez was first explored by Captain W.R. Abercrombie of the U.S. Army in 1899. His goal was to locate a practical route for linking Eagle, then a thriving gold rush settlement and port for steamboats on the Yukon, with the salt-water, ice-free port of Valdez on the Pacific tidewater of Prince William Sound.

Following the gold strike at Fairbanks after the turn of the century and as Fairbanks grew, a new wagon trail was built from the confluence of the Copper and Gulkana rivers south of the Alaska Range northwest to Fairbanks. Today's Richardson Highway generally follows the route of this wagon road and for the last 98 miles to Fairbanks joins with the Alaska Highway.

Top
The visitor center at Tok. Tourism contributes significantly to the economy at Tok, a trade and service center for all types of transportation and a major overland point of entry for the state.
(Sharon Paul, Staff, reprinted from *The MILEPOST*®)

Above
North Pole (population 823), Santa's headquarters in Alaska. In 1944 Bon Davis homesteaded the North Pole area. Dahl and Gaske Development Company bought the Davis homestead and subdivided it. They decided to name the settlement North Pole, hoping to attract a toy manufacturer who would advertise his products as being made at the North Pole.
(Nancy Simmerman)

Black Rapids Lodge, one of the roadhouses of the Richardson Highway, 137 miles southeast of Fairbanks. To the west of the highway near here is Black Rapids Glacier, which suddenly advanced on a front over a mile wide in 1936. By the time the glacier halted its forward movement in 1940, it had advanced four miles from its former terminus.
(Nancy Simmerman)

THE TAYLOR HIGHWAY

The 161-mile Taylor Highway (Alaska Route 5), runs from Tetlin Junction on the Alaska Highway to Eagle on the Yukon River. At Jack Wade junction it meets the Klondike Loop highway coming from Dawson City, Yukon Territory, to the east. In part the highway follows the valley of the Fortymile River, a hub of early gold mining activity.

Above
The Taylor Highway is gold mining country as this abandoned dredge at Jack Wade testifies. Jack Wade is the junction where Canada's Klondike Loop joins the Taylor Highway.
(Gil Mull, reprinted from *The MILEPOST®*)

Top
At the end of the Taylor Highway, where it reaches the Yukon River, is Eagle, population about 200, a historic community undertaking a program to restore many of its fine old structures. The town hall, community well and several residences are visible in this photo.
(Gil Mull, reprinted from *ALASKA®* magazine)

Above
Dee Corbin keeps an eye on the post office at Chicken. The post office was established in 1903 to serve a mining community.
(George Wuerthner)

THE STEESE HIGHWAY

The Steese Highway begins at Fairbanks. For part of its 162 miles it follows prospectors' trails in what was once a highly important gold mining area. The road was opened for automobiles in the 1920's and named for General James G. Steese, U.S. Army, a former president of the Alaska Road Commission. The Steese Highway ends at Circle, 50 miles south of the Arctic Circle and 1,680 miles from the North Pole. This community is the northernmost point in the country that can be reached by automobile, traveling on a public road—until or unless the North Slope Haul Road is opened to the public beyond the Yukon River.

Chena Hot Springs Road, off the Steese Highway 5 miles north of Fairbanks, makes a 55-mile side trip through rolling farmlands and hillsides covered with spruce, birch, aspen, tamarack and alder.

Right
A portion of the Davidson Ditch, Alaska's first elevated pipeline, passes near the Steese Highway about 60 miles north of Fairbanks. Built in 1925 by the Fairbanks Exploration Company to carry the water used to float gold dredges, the 83-mile-long ditch, begins near the Steese and ends near Fox. The system is a combination of ditches and inverted siphons across the valleys. Originally there were 15 siphons, totaling six miles of pipeline. Their diameter varied from 46 to 56 inches and they could carry 56,100 gallons per minute. After the dredges closed, the water was used for power until 1967, when a flood destroyed a 150-foot bridge and flattened 700 to 1,000 feet of pipe.
(Gil Mull)

Below
This log house greets visitors to Central (population about 70), a former rest stop on the trail to Circle. Central is situated on Crooked Creek and spreads along the Steese Highway.
(Gil Mull)

Left
At the end of the Chena Hot Springs Road is an area of geothermal activity first reported in 1907 by the U.S. Geological Survey. The springs take their name from the nearby Chena River, which flows southwest toward Fairbanks.
(Dave Johnson)

83

THE ELLIOTT HIGHWAY

Alaska Route 2, the Elliott Highway, branches off from the Steese Highway 11 miles north of Fairbanks. The Elliott then winds 152 miles through gold mining country to Manley Hot Springs. Access to the White Mountain Trail System, an 80-mile hiking route, is from this highway about 13 miles out from Fox, a community at the junction of the Elliott and Steese highways. Poppies, blueberries, relics from early gold mining efforts — the Elliott offers a fine view of the Interior.

Above
Saws, pans, lanterns and an assortment of other gadgets hang from this outbuilding at Livengood.
(Don and Afton Blanc)

Right
Livengood (population 110), four miles from the junction of the Elliott Highway and the North Slope Haul Road, served as a mining camp in the early days and as the site of a pipeline construction camp during the mid-1970's.
(Nancy Simmerman)

Above
The Elliott Highway winds north and west of Fairbanks to Manley Hot Springs (population 74). In 1902 J.F. Karshner established a homestead here about the same time that the U.S. Signal Corps set up a telegraph station nearby. Frank Manley built a four-story hotel in the village in 1907 but it was not until 1957 that the town changed its name from Baker Hot Springs to Manley Hot Springs.
(Gil Mull)

Right
The airstrip at Manley Hot Springs.
(Sharon Paul, Staff, reprinted from *The MILEPOST®*)

THE NORTH SLOPE HAUL ROAD

The 416-mile North Slope Haul Road begins four miles west of Livengood on the Elliott Highway and ends at Prudhoe Bay on the arctic coast. The road was built as part of the trans-Alaska pipeline project with construction starting on April 29, 1974. Five months later the road stretched 360 miles from Prudhoe to the Yukon River. The portion from the Yukon to the Elliott Highway had been built earlier. Three million man-hours were required to construct the 28-foot-wide road which has a minimum gravel base of three feet and deepens to five or six feet in less stable soil. A private company turned the road over to the state of Alaska in 1978, leaving state officials to decide how to manage this latest addition to the highway system, which remained closed to the public in 1979.

Left
The trans-Alaska pipeline and North Slope Haul Road wind north across the Interior from this point near Livengood.
(Robert Langlotz)

Right
The North Slope Haul Road crosses the Yukon River 56 miles north of the Elliott Highway. Public access to the haul road ends at the far end of the bridge. Only vehicles with special permits may proceed farther.
(Sharon Paul, Staff, reprinted from *The MILEPOST*®)

THE GEORGE PARKS HIGHWAY

In 1971, when this 358-mile addition to
Alaska's highway system was completed,
it was known as the Anchorage-Fairbanks
Highway and was designated Alaska
Route 3. Later, in 1975, the route was offi-
cially renamed in honor of George A.
Parks, territorial governor from 1925 to
1933. The road enters the Interior near
Mount McKinley National Park and
descends from the Alaska Range through
the rolling, timbered countryside to
Fairbanks.

The Major Attraction: Mount McKinley National Park

To some it is Denali—the Great One. To others it is Mount McKinley. For the people of the Interior it is the ever-present giant on their southern flank: Mount McKinley, at 20,320 feet the crown of the Alaska Range and the highest peak in North America.

Inspired by the enthusiasm and persistence of naturalist Charles Sheldon, various officials of the territorial and federal governments agreed to support establishment of a national park in the mountains and foothills surrounding the Great One. On February 16, 1917, nine years after Sheldon first proposed the sanctuary, President Woodrow Wilson signed the bill creating Mount McKinley National Park in honor of President William McKinley.

Some of those interested in the area have proposed changing the park's name to Denali. So far, however, the U.S. Board of Geographic Names has not officially sanctioned the change.

Today, Mount McKinley National Park is a 3,029.5-square-mile haven for numerous large mammals, smaller fur bearers, myriad birds, colorful wild flowers, and thousands of tourists who come to enjoy the Interior's major attraction.

Mount Brooks, 11,940 feet

Mount Silverthrone, 13,200 feet

Calm waters of a tundra pond reflect the images of Mount McKinley and peaks of the Alaska Range to the east, photographed from Camp Denali.
(Ed Scherockman, reprinted from *A Tourist Guide to Mount McKinley*)

North Peak of Mount McKinley, 19,470 feet

South Peak of Mount McKinley, 20,320 feet (Main summit, two miles between South and North Peaks.)

Mount Carpe, 12,550 feet

Browne Tower, 14,600 feet

Wickersham Wall, over 14,000 feet vertical rise from base.

Mount Tatum, 11,140 feet

Mount Koven, 12,210 feet

Karstens Ridge, 11,000 to 14,000 feet

Right
Thousands of visitors come to the park on the
Alaska Railroad which stops near the park
hotel. In 1978 officials at McKinley recorded
460,624 total visits.
(Gary Brown)

Below
Tour buses from Mount McKinley Hotel stop at
Stony Hill overlook.
(Johnny Johnson)

Right
The Nenana River, which forms the eastern
park boundary, is just the place to try
whitewater kayaking. On a Fourth of July
weekend more than a dozen contestants vied
for places in the Nenana Whitewater Classic.
(Mark Kelley)

Far right
McKinley is also a haven for the Interior's
mightiest pest, the mosquito. These hikers
are prepared, however, with homemade
mosquito nets.
(Rick McIntyre)

A band of Dall sheep ewes and lambs keeps an eye on a McKinley Park shuttle bus. The Park Service provides free rides aboard shuttle buses which stop often for wildlife photos and pick up or let off passengers wherever they wish—except in restricted areas. Park visitors may drive their own vehicles to designated camping spots beyond the Savage River checkpoint (Mile 12 of the park highway) after obtaining camping permits at the Riley Creek visitor information center. (Ron Lambert)

A photographer tries to capture on film the grandeur of this unnamed canyon in the Alaska Range. (Martin Grosnick)

Above
The challenge—climbing the highest peak in North America. This party is descending Karstens Ridge, at the 14,000-foot level, in July.
(Johnny Johnson)

Below
The Great One generates its own weather and storms can come up without warning. These climbers are digging in at the 14,00-foot level in June.
(Johnny Johnson)

During the winter, the National Park Service patrols the back country of McKinley with dog teams. Dog mushing in the park is a tradition that originated with Harry Karstens, the park's first superintendent. He set up patrols to discourage poaching of the abundant animal life in the park. With the addition of modern communication equipment, the patrols continue today much as they did in the 1920's under Karstens.

Sturdy sleds *(above)* are constructed to haul supplies in McKinley's back country.
Left—About 28 dogs live at the park's kennels. This pup is getting its toenails trimmed.
Right—On patrol in McKinley's back country.
(All by Gary Brown; photo at right reprinted from *ALASKA*® magazine)

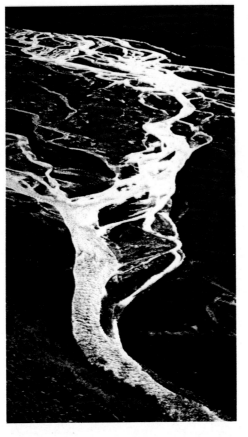

Left
The wolf, one of the more controversial mammals in some areas of the Interior, enjoys the same protected status of the other animals in McKinley. There are several wolf packs within the park and it is left to nature to maintain the prey/predator balance.
(Stephen Krasemann)

Left
A hoary marmot must keep an eye out for predators while it gathers nest grass. Talus slopes are the perfect habitat for marmots. When disturbed, the marmots emit a high-pitched whistle.
(Stephen Krasemann)

Below
Three bull caribou en route to the rutting grounds pass through Thorofare Pass.
(Martin Grosnick)

Right
Care to get any closer? An eye-to-eye view of a Toklat grizzly.
(Stephen Krasemann, reprinted from *ALASKA*® magazine)

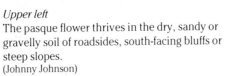

Upper left
The pasque flower thrives in the dry, sandy or gravelly soil of roadsides, south-facing bluffs or steep slopes.
(Johnny Johnson)

Left
Tundra in the park as well as in other areas of the Interior can be covered with a major hindrance to speedy hiking . . . hummocks. These soft, spongy, unstable bumps in the tundra make for tricky footing.
(Ed Cooper)

Above
Braided stream channels of the East Fork of the Toklat River.
(Ed Cooper)

Mount McKinley at sunrise, viewed from Wonder Lake.
(Ed Cooper)

Fairbanks Today

*O*n winter nights when the green aurora pulses in the skies over Fairbanks, Neal B. Brown of the University of Alaska's Geophysical Institute drives north along the Steese Highway, past the Felix Pedro monument, past Cleary Summit with its ski slopes, down through the valley and past the weathered gray buildings of the Chatanika gold camp which still cling to the hillside there.

Just beyond lies Poker Flat, a rustic assemblage of nondescript buildings stuffed with some of the world's most sophisticated equipment, designed to explore the earth's envelope and space itself. Brown is range supervisor for the Poker Flat Research Range, with the complicated job of troubleshooting and nursing and facilitating the work there, which draws scientists from all over the world, each engaged in one or another aspect of one of man's most persistent curiosities: what lies beyond our small planet.

At Poker Flat, the frontier is the alchemical mystery of space itself. But its workers wear the Fairbanks plaid shirt and the atmosphere is devastatingly casual, punctuated by brief moments of glory when the rockets whoosh off.

The work at Poker Flat is just one of the projects of the university's world-famous Geophysical Institute. Its new director, Dr. Juan G. Roederer has a com-

Above
If it's true that you have to have a sense of humor to be content in Fairbanks, then the owner of this car is happy, indeed. Fairbanksans also appear to be born optimists, despite the city's occasional setbacks. As city manager Wally Droz says about the outlook of townspeople toward the future, "If we can't do it today, we'll do it tomorrow."
(Tom Walker)

Right
A springtime overview of Fairbanks, in the broad Tanana River valley.
(Randy Brandon,
Third Eye Photography)

manding vision of the role of this institute: "Alaska is one of the most remarkable places on the earth's surface. It is a giant, natural geophysical laboratory that offers virtually unparalleled opportunities to the inquiring mind to find out about our planet Earth, about the bounty it offers and about the threats it occasionally poses to mankind."

It may seem a long way from this point to the moment each summer when at the start of Fairbanks's Golden Days festival, a representative Felix Pedro, clutching a gold poke and followed by a mule, makes a bewildered trek down Cushman Street in imitation of a real Felix Pedro who in 1903 came in from the creeks just outside a fledgling Fairbanks with his news of a gold strike. But there are connections, both psychic and physical. Here he is, everyman, with a discovery in his hand, for better or for worse.

The problem with trying to tell what is Fairbanks is just this mix of the pragmatic with the dream. It's less a geography than it is an organism. It is among other things, a center, a hub and not only for the roads *some*, (not all) Fairbanksans have been dreaming about for years, but also for ideas. Thus, the Delta barley project originated here in the mind of Fairbanks lawyer Ed Merdes.

Or take the North Commission, which dreamed big dreams of a road or a railroad to the just-discovered Prudhoe Bay oil fields. In 1967, it commissioned engineer Jim Dalton to survey a railbed from Nenana north. Heading out in -50°F weather, Dalton pressed through almost to Bettles Field before bringing the enterprise to a halt.

But the dream was not ended. In 1970 and 1971, it materialized again in the form of the "Ice Road"— briefly named "The Hickel Highway"—which followed old mining trails and roads straight north and

up the John River through Anaktuvuk Pass to the slope. It too had a brief life, and was eventually replaced by the present Haul Road. But those who traveled with the cat trains and ate hot meals from the cook shacks remember it was a lot more than a road. The men thought they were making history.

The principals in these adventures were Fairbanksans, mostly by residence, but in some cases by inclination. They were establishment types, well-respected, well-known solid citizens and this is the point. It is as characteristic of Fairbanks as its fabled ice fog that every man is nursing an idea and figuring

Trucks rumble north along the ice road to the North Slope in 1970, before construction of the trans-Alaska pipeline. The road's replacement—the North Slope Haul Road—has been turned over to the state by Alyeska Pipeline Service Company and many Fairbanksans hope it will be opened for use by the public . . . a move that would stimulate the local economy.
(Jane Pender)

An aerial wide-angle view of downtown Fairbanks in spring, with the still-frozen Chena River curving through the left-center of the photo. This view was taken from a hot-air balloon, and shows Minnie Street in the foreground, with Wendell Avenue Crossing the Chena River and heading toward the downtown area.
(Alan Paulson)

out how to make it work and confident it will. This may be what sociologists identify as a "frontier mentality." Whatever it's called, it's real. Define it today in terms of Chuck Reese's South Fairbanks Industrial Park, or Paul Gavora's Shopping Malls, or Bob Hufman's stubborn, patient explorations of energy alternatives, or Celia Hunter's pristine wilderness; or Joe

Joe Usibelli stands in front of a monster dragline.
(Jane Pender)

Bob Hufman, manager of Golden Valley Electric Association in Fairbanks. The co-op built a mine-mouth coal-fired plant at Healy which now produces 25,000 kw of electricity for the Interior.
(Jane Pender)

The rich veins of the Usibelli Coal Mine near Healy. Presently the only coal mine operating commercially in Alaska, Usibelli produces about 700,000 tons of coal annually and has been in operation since 1918.
(Ed Cooper)

Usibelli's strip mine, which he turned into a game preserve.

Or maybe a better symbol might be Fairbanks's own particular variety of establishment activist: Pete Haggland, pilot. The slow-speaking, thoughtful son of one of Fairbanks's fabled doctors, young Pete rose to the D-2 challenge with street marches, lobbies and Alaskans Unite. A little surprised, maybe, at what he's

continued on page 102

A Dall sheep ewe and lamb wander among the reseeded hillsides of the mine. A band of 150 sheep feeds on the grasses each spring.
(Kenneth R. Kollodge)

Usibelli Coal
POWER AND ENERGY AT HEALY

The Fairbanks area has produced tilters-at-windmills and tempers-of-fate. Might be the climate; might be the prediliction for the more remote spots of the world; might just be a gambler's instinct.

Whatever, the most recent candidates are a home-grown pair: Joe Usibelli of Healy and Bob Hufman of Fairbanks: Mr. Coal Mine and Mr. Golden Valley Electric Co-op, known locally as GVEA. In both cases, the windmill is the same: federal obstruction of what seems to both to be legitimate and necessary enterprise.

Joe Usibelli's entire life has been oriented around a coal mine at Healy, the only operating coal mine in the state, which produces subbituminous coal with a sulphur content of one-quarter of one percent—a valuable commodity in a world running out of oil. Hufman in 1967 put a mine-mouth power plant at Healy to utilize the coal mined there, and to bring electric power to Fairbanks and to rural areas between Fairbanks and Healy. These enterprises were at the time considered both prudent and canny.

Over the years, Usibelli showed signs of being ahead of his time. In 1971, he began seeding the strip-mined area of the Healy valley with grasses and fertilizer—all on his own, and without government fiat, and by now has restored the valley to a very nearly pristine state. At least, it's pristine enough that 150 Dall sheep come down out of the surrounding hills to fatten on the grasses each spring. He also, all on his own, had the state declare the valley a game refuge. No hunting is allowed in the Healy valley—an environmentalist's dream, one might think: the strip-mining operation proceeding side by side with revegetation and Dall sheep, moose and wolves, and a host of smaller animals, a kind of technological Eden.

Unhappily, along came the Surface Mining Control and Reclamation Act of 1977, 1,000 pages of regulations which now threaten to either regulate Usibelli out of business or at least to complicate his operation considerably.

Samples: Usibelli reseeds with 70 pounds of grasses per acre combined with the needed fertilizers for his acres, which do not produce much topsoil. These grasses provide both broad and deep root structures which lock what soil there is in place, and in a few years provide happy habitation for native plants which are now

establishing themselves there in increasing numbers. Problem: the new regulations insist he must seed with native seeds, ignoring the Alaskan facts that such seeds are never collected here in anywhere near the quantity he requires, and that further, many native plants use forms of propagation other than seeds.

So far, it's a stand-off, but there's more. Usibelli is also required by these regulations to clean up ground water—not water that's used in settling ponds or elsewhere in his operation, just ground water—to 35 mg/liter of suspended particles. Destination of this nearly drinkable water: the Nenana River which in its natural, or pristine state, carries 3,000 to 11,000 mg/liter of these self-same suspended particles. There are more such regulations, but you get the drift.

The second windmill tilter is Bob Hufman, similarly frustrated. Take that wonderful low-sulphur coal he uses to power his power plant. It compares favorably to East Coast coal, which averages 4% to 5% sulphur and really does need to be cleaned up. You'd think EPA would be happy with what the good Lord produced in Healy, but not so. Instead, they are insisting that Hufman remove 85% of that already minute one quarter of one percent sulphur—even though no technology exists to do this. And even though plants which use the East Coast high-sulphur coal, even after expensive treatment, still emit larger amounts of sulphur than the Healy plant does before treatment.

Another question has to do with particle emission. Healy is a windy spot and whatever particles emit from the smokestack vanish very rapidly. But, there's Mount McKinley National Park just down

the way 20 miles or so. If GVEA installs a high smokestack, the emissions might pollute that pristine air. If on the other hand, they put in a shorter smokestack, then areas near the plant might be subject to pollution. In both cases, the operative word is might, not will, or does. Local residents think the wind in the area is enough to thoroughly dissipate any emissions, but never mind. The solution now is the installation of a complex, $5 million "bag house" which precipitates the emissions. That keeps Healy No. 1 on line, at least for the moment, though the electricity costs a lot more. Unhappily, the cost effectiveness has also brought about a side effect: cancellation of a proposed second power plant for the area, to have been called Healy No. 2. Reason: cost of this plant would have been in excess of $280 million and the energy produced would have been 7½¢/kilowatt at the plant.

"Ridiculous," says Hufman.

Adds Usibelli: "Environmental regulation could result in energy costing so much that the ordinary consumer would not be able to afford it." And, adds this normally optimistic man: "I'm scared. I really think we're regulating ourselves right into the ground." —*Jane Pender*

Lower left
A truck dumps its load down the chute that separates the coal according to size.

Below
A coal truck delivers the valuable mineral to the rail car loading chute at Healy.
(Both photos by Mark Kelley)

doing. He seems more comfortable on those cold nights when he flies his plane across the silent snowy Interior landscape and he likes to swing his plane around to take a better look at Neal Brown's aurora.

See how it is here? Neal Brown's aurora; Pete Haggland's rebellion. In Fairbanks, nothing is faceless or anonymous or mass produced. Every project has a name, everybody is reachable. These are the folks

between people. And here, the legislators are accessible—state, borough and city. People can go directly." He pauses, then adds thoughtfully, "It takes endurance." This is not a criticism, it's a statement of fact.

Droz has been into city politics since the early 1960's. In and out. Retired once. He managed the Municipal Utilities department for a while, and now is

who sit on the boards and the councils, who run the stores and build the hospital, who create an expensive, stylish library that fits like an old shoe. City and school board and borough meetings here are often marathons—with their diverse visions, Fairbanksans are born arguers who don't hesitate to speak up and they turn out in droves to be heard.

Or they do the same individually, on the phone. Straight to the top. Borough Mayor John Carlson hears every, or *most* every local complaint about the borough animal shelter, the dump, the borough taxes.

City Manager Wally Droz puts that more generally, speaking of how receptive the borough and the city are to suggestions. "They listen to people, try to cooperate," he says. "There's direct communication

back as city manager. A sophisticated, shirt-sleeved man who talks about office buildings and revitalizing downtown and the peculiar, particular Fairbanks problems such as unification: "The largest part of the borough is rural. You've got people living out there because they want to. They don't want to be involved with government looking over their shoulder, and they would be the first ones to not want unification and there's nothing wrong with that."

And there's Carlson, a 30-year resident whose voice inexplicably sounds like Smokey the Bear, but whose ideas are vintage Fairbanks. The Haul Road: "I want to see it open." Petrochemicals: "We've been talking about a gas conditioning plant here. They've talked about that up on the slope. We say they ought

102

to have it here in Fairbanks—burn coal here. Up on the slope they use 60% of the gas to process the other 40%. So why not process it here where they could burn coal? Fact is, I'm gonna get hold of Joe Usibelli and sit down and talk to him about that."

The conditioning plant is not just John Carlson's. It's the largest floating idea in the Fairbanks of the seventies, especially since the installation of the Earth Resources refinery at North Pole—the one which brought planes of Japan Air Lines and Korean Airlines to Fairbanks to be refueled.

Mayor Bill Wood of Fairbanks is a philosopher of "value-added," among other things. "The gas at Prudhoe Bay or at Cook Inlet as it comes out of the ground at wellhead has an X value. When it is processed through basic chemistry it has about a 7X value. When it goes through other stages it goes up to 34, 67, 120, and when it finally gets through the highly specialized synthetics and plastics, it can be as much as 240 or more X times the value of the raw material itself. What seems so silly to me is that in our state we have ignored this principle and we've gone for the lowest possible price of X—the price just out of the ground—and thrown away the 240 X."

Chuck Reese, entrepreneur of the South Fairbanks Industrial Park, has embroidered the thought, comparing the possible location of a conditioning plant here with the initial bonding issue of a port for Anchorage, which served as a catalyst for development of that city.

Says Reese: "The petrochemical industries are basically quite clean and are tremendously capital intensive and we already have enough interest exhibited here that if we even went to just the breaking down of the different components of gas here. . . . The old Haines pipeline (built by the military and now retired) is capable of taking all of the propane gas and getting it to tidewater at very little cost as far as rehabilitating the line. There certainly is an ample supply of tank cars available so that the railroad could be the connection to take the other gasses to export markets."

Nobody in Fairbanks likes the term "boom or bust,"

which has been used for years to describe the local economy. Droz says the community is in a "holding pattern" until something develops on the gas pipeline, and some such circumlocution, uncharacteristic in this call-a-spade-a-spade community, is in general use here.

An observer, however, does perceive such a pattern. Fairbanks is a shirt-sleeve town, but the pace here is not that of any manufacturing or steel town, at least in normal times. Instead, the peculiar rhythm here is more like that of the Point Hope or Barrow whalers. Feast or famine, hard work and party, work followed by sometimes very protracted temporary retirement. By any name, it's not stable and that is

Students walk between classes in February on the University of Alaska campus. Dominating this view is the Gruening Building, near the heart of the hillside campus.
(Mark Kelley)

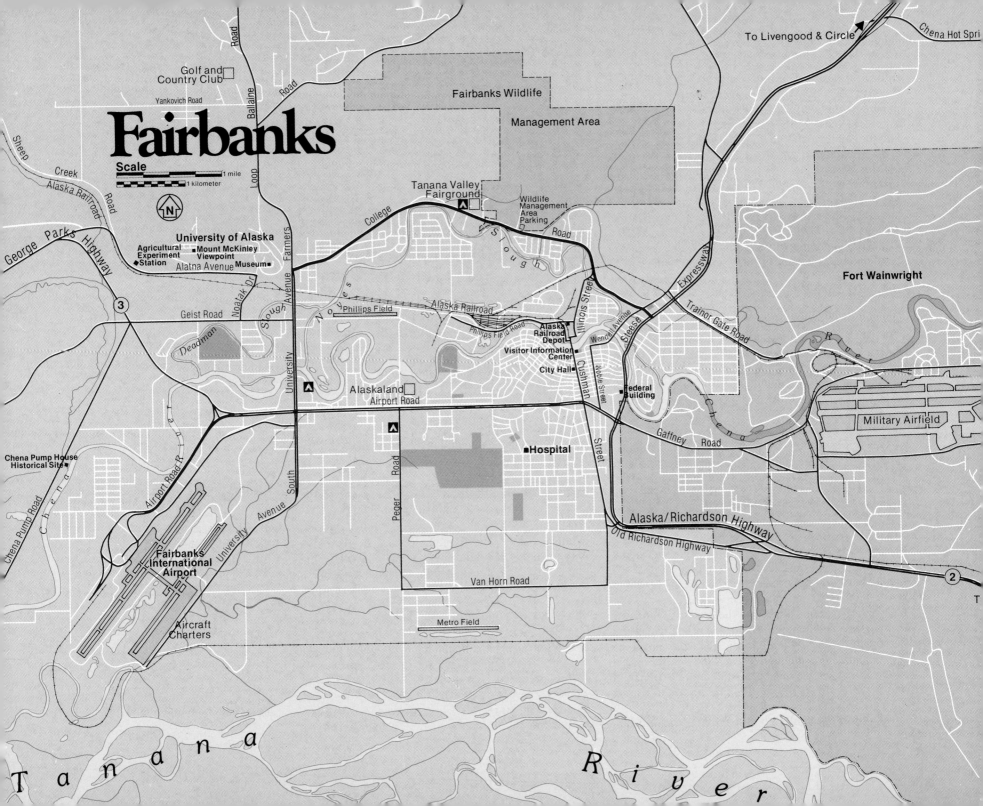

Fairbanks

Scale
1 mile
1 kilometer

N

Golf and Country Club

Yankovich Road

Fairbanks Wildlife

Management Area

Sheep Creek Road

Alaska Railroad

Ballaine Road

Loop

Tanana Valley Fairground

Wildlife Management Area Parking

Road

George Parks Highway

University of Alaska
Agricultural Experiment Station

Mount McKinley Viewpoint

Museum

Alatna Avenue

College

Noatak Dr

Slough Avenue

Farmers

Noyes

Slough

Illinois Street

Steese Expressway

Fort Wainwright

3

Geist Road

Phillips Field

Alaska Railroad

Phillips Field Road

Alaska Railroad Depot

Visitor Information Center

City Hall

Wendell Avenue

Steese

Cushman

Trainor Gate Road

Chena River

Deadman

Alaskaland

Airport Road

Noble Street

Federal Building

Gaffney Road

Military Airfield

Chena Pump House Historical Site

Airport Road R

University Avenue

South

Peger Road

Street

Hospital

Chena

Alaska/Richardson Highway

Old Richardson Highway

2

Fairbanks International Airport

University Avenue

Van Horn Road

Aircraft Charters

Metro Field

To Livengood & Circle

Chena Hot Spri

T

Tanana River

Chena

Chena River

what all the local brainstorming is about: to get some kind of a year-round, year-after-year base here. Still, to go with that, there's also the Fairbanks axiom that either the winters or the busts "tends to weed 'em out." If you're a Fairbanksan you're a survivor—sour grapes maybe, but a survivor.

Meantime, the organism proceeds in its own leisurely fashion. Droz says accurately, "In Fairbanks, if we can't do it today we'll do it tomorrow."

On the whole, the community rather enjoyed the pipeline boom. Well, in a way. There was much complaining about the traffic and in particular those yellow Alyeska trucks which turned the 10 blocks of downtown Cushman Street into a sluggish marathon. Neither did people like the lines in supermarkets or the increased pace which speeded up the Fairbanks slow stroll. But the money rolled in and rolled in and there was a lot of home building and new faces, and for a gaudy time there were new restaurants and that free circus on Two Street. People paid off their mortgages and bought property and built dream houses and went into business and three new shopping malls started up out of the midtown . . . and the downtown went into a decline.

But Fairbanks is not an easily killable organism. After a period of complaining and criticism, the downtown began to revive. Now it's been redecorated with murals on the sides and fronts of buildings, done by CETA workers under a miniscule $35,000 grant.

Fairbanks is often criticized for its rustic atmosphere, its unfashionable citizens, its lack of urbanity . . . but it's hard to be cosmopolitan when it's 50 below . . .

There's a kind of northern San Francisco feel to it, Fairbanks-style, that is. The downtown gaps are slowly being filled in with tiny Ma and Pa operations, craft and specialty shops, doing business in old houses on shoestrings. To go with this, Cook Inlet Native Association is now exploring ways to redo the splendid old art deco post office building which was abandoned for a more efficient one last year.

And there are the expansions Droz talks about: Penneys and First National Bank, a new City Hall—three stories of parking garage, three of offices, with possible participation of the borough. What he sees is a movement of the city core to an area already occupied by the fire and police department, the court building, the state office building and Nordstrom's. "They're even talking about overhead walkways to connect these buildings," Droz says. He thinks this kind of development will revitalize the downtown.

But it's growth more than development. Characteristically enough, Fairbanksans have responded coolly to proposals which would have turned the downtown into a fake frontier for the tourist trade.

The town doesn't work that way. Just as Chuck Reese is talking of reviving the old Haines pipeline, so the town itself incorporates its past and puts it to work instead of stuffing it for a museum. Years ago as part of the little empire of one of Fairbanks's more fabled citizens, Austin E. "Cap" Lathrop, a giant pipe organ was installed in a movie theatre called The Empress, on Second Avenue. In time The Empress went out of business, but the old organ was saved over all the years and has recently been installed in a modern eatery where it is fondly played by organ afficionadoes from all over—including Dr. Juan Roederer of the Geophysical Institute.

And just down the street from this restaurant is another similarly utilized relic of the past: what's left of the old Nevada Bar, displaced from First Avenue, now enlivens the style of "The Big Eye"—the International Hotel.

Fairbanks is often criticized for its rustic atmosphere, its unfashionable citizens, its lack of urbanity. It's like a market town, to which the agricultural folk bring their wares, some say. It's far from cosmopolitan: it's hard to be cosmopolitan when it's 50 below, as it often is in the long Fairbanks winter.

Yet, it shelters a population which is extraordinarily diverse, not only ethnically but also in terms of the lifestyles. And it's a town that extends itself hospitably to accommodate each. Surprisingly flexible, if you think of the town as being politically conservative to right wing, which the elections demonstrate. But that conservatism does not mean insularity. The winter and summer solstices are nearly counter-culture events, demonstrations of folksy craft and individual art and lifestyles, and they are popular with everyone. The blooming of the downtown with paint and art is not characteristic of a fixed and backward-looking conservative community.

On the other hand, Fairbanks supports what is

Diane Binkley prepares to jump-start her truck in downtown Fairbanks. Vehicles often are kept warm during cold winter months with headbolt-heater units, plugged into electrical outlets in some parking lots. Radio-dispatched car-starting services do a brisk business when the temperature drops into the -30 °F to -50 °F range.
(Robert Langlotz)

107

often thought of as the bastion of small town America: sports. Little League and Little Dribblers, stock cars, horses, dog racing, curling, soccer, swimming, basketball, baseball, biking and hiking, motorboats and snow machines and rafts and canoes and weekends out on some gravel pit up on the trans-Alaska pipeline road, or fishing in some obscure creek, or prospecting or walking over ridges or berry picking or hunting. And also: The Fairbanks Light Opera Company and the Fairbanks Drama Association, and a thousand clubs and lodges and groups and

Wintertime Fairbanks

In Fairbanks, the turning of the seasons is an important event marked by summer and winter solstice fairs, a fall equinox marathon and the annual Winter Carnival—a particularly festive event that is scheduled each March.

By March the sun has returned to the skies, temperatures have risen to a tolerable point and winter sports are in full swing—cross-country skiing, snowshoeing, snowmobiling, skating, curling, hockey and the like.

The Winter Carnival involves all of these sports and more—notably the running of the North American Sled Dog Championships. Other carnival events include snow-sculpture contests, amusement rides, pancake feeds, chili-eating contests and more.

a hundred diverse churches and the pioneers and old houses with their lavish gardens and trees trimmed with frost rime in winter side by side with condominiums, and in the hills, the big expensive pipeline houses next door to the environmentalists' 8-by-10-foot cabins.

Fairbanks welcomed the fast food emporiums which sprang up on Airport Way before and after the pipeline as enthusiastically as it did the new malls. But even though some of these structures look as though they have been cast in plastic, they have not really affected the style of the town, which remains diverse

continued on page 110

108

Clockwise from above

► Wintertime activities haven't changed a great deal in Fairbanks. Here early-day ice skaters glide around a rink on the frozen Chena River, while curling enthusiasts occupy the center of the impromptu arena.
(Reprinted from *The Alaska Sportsman®*)

► Curling enthusiasts clear off a portion of the Chena River, in downtown Fairbanks, for a match in early spring. The game involves two teams with four players on each side, attempting to slide heavy curling stones across the ice into circular targets.
(Mark Kelley)

► Snow machines race around an oval track on the Chena River during the annual Fairbanks Winter Carnival, held in March and coinciding with the running of the North American Sled Dog Championships.
(Ron Lambert)

► Each spring students at the University of Alaska attempt to out-do each other with elaborate ice sculptures. In 1979 a group of future engineers created this ice arch.
(Alan Paulson)

► Olive Anderson models the fur parka that has just won a fur fashion contest during festivities in Fairbanks.
(Robert Langlotz)

► A crowd of about 350 cross-country skiers races uphill at the start of the 30-kilometer Skiathon, a March event in Fairbanks.
(Tom Walker)

► Harvey Drake mushes down Second Avenue during the North American Sled Dog Championships, one of the biggest wintertime events in Fairbanks.
(Tom Walker)

The riverboat *Discovery* operates daily on the Chena and Tanana rivers during summer months, offering visitors a look at the Interior's paddlewheeler past. Captain Jim Binkley, skipper of the *Discovery*, comes from a long-time riverboating family—his father, Captain Charles Binkley, designed, built and skippered sternwheelers in the early days on the Yukon and Stikine rivers.
(Tim Thompson)

and hand-crafted, unless you prefer homemade, which better describes the fact that houses here—like the town itself—just keep growing, to the despair of the zoners and the planners.

Where is the town going? How is the community developing? What's its future?

Sometimes it feels as if Fairbanks is everything half the community wants, with an antsy other half driving to make something else of it, a conflict most recently demonstrated when urban dwellers told borough planners they wanted more services, and the rural people said all they wanted was to be left alone.

Says Chuck Reese, "Fairbanks sits right here in the center of the state. It's the take-off point to the slope, it's the terminus of the Alaska Railroad; it's the mid-point of the supply route to Valdez or to Prudhoe Bay. It's the terminus or starting point of the Haines pipe-line, which is a viable pipeline to tidewater. It enjoys a tremendous tax base by virtue of the pipeline and the refinery that's already existing. These are things that an industry coming in really looks for. It's the most natural sleeping beauty you've ever seen, and it's just waiting for the crown prince to give it a little kiss and away it will go. . . ."

On the other hand, Mayor Wood sees Fairbanks as the center of an Alaska he describes as "the keystone of the world's most dynamic trading area, the Pacific basin." He says Alaska is central to the developing nations that border the Pacific Ocean, pointing out that "over 60% of the known reserves of all resources are in countries that border the Pacific. Two-thirds of all the people in the world live in nations that border the Pacific. Geographically we sit in a strategic position: we are the air crossroads of the whole Pacific region.

Clockwise from below

► Fairbanks has quite a collection of unusual clubs and groups, including the Midnight Sun Moosehiders and Muzzleloaders Association. This member is participating in one of the club's regular meets.
(Tom Walker)

► Kathy Kollodge and John Kohler of Fairbanks perform in Neil Simon's *The Last of the Red Hot Lovers.* Fairbanksans are extremely active in theater, with dramas and musicals being staged throughout the year by the Fairbanks Drama Association, Fairbanks Light Opera Theater, University of Alaska theater department, Alaska Repertory Theater, Laughing Stock and area high schools.
(Kenneth R. Kollodge)

► Hunting and fishing are important to many residents in the Interior and contribute substantially to the local economy in Fairbanks—via outdoor clothing stores, sporting-goods shops, air charter services . . . and even taxidermies. Skip Scott, of Alpine Taxidermy, puts the finishing touches on a bull caribou mount.
(Tom Walker)

Our resources tend to complement and are needed on the Asian side and we are in the geographic and strategic position to serve the whole Pacific Rim. We have an advantage none of the other nation-states have. We don't have much population, but that population is highly educated and considerably above the average in technical and scientific sophistication.''

And yet, always in Fairbanks, there is the contrast. One of the more recent buildings in the downtown is that of Doyon, Inc., which also houses the nonprofit corporation, Tanana Chiefs Conference (TCC), devoted to the delivery of services of the federal government to the 43 villages in its area which surrounds Fairbanks and the borough.

Spud Williams, president of TCC, details its work: health aides, agricultural specialists, subregional administrators, secretarial help. And program specialists and support staff. About 200 persons altogether, some 60 in Fairbanks and the rest located in the villages. But here, the dream is far from Chuck Reese's dream of a big city, bigger than Anchorage, someday. "The function of the Fairbanks office is changing very radically this year and more so next," says Williams, "in that we're subregionalizing the whole organization . . . cutting down the [Fairbanks] staff to just technical assistance in most of the program areas and putting most of the service delivery out into the villages on a subregional basis. Each subregion will also have an advisory board. That will cut the Fairbanks office down to about 40 employees . . . but you know the nature of the beast of the bureaucracy . . . you get rid of one and you bring in two."

It can't be done, one thinks. The town cannot be defined except one by one, because despite its growth, everybody still contrives to know everybody else, and so the diversity is personal.

Only one thing seems abundantly clear: it's a topsy town, "jes' growin'," a family town, which might realize its promise, or might not. It's a town that is not for everyone, but deeply satisfying to those who have figured out how to survive and thrive on what it dishes out.
—*Jane Pender*

People of the Interior

*E*xtremes of temperature: bitterly cold, dark winters alternating with the endless hot days of summer. Chronic economic problems. Constant political controversy. Few roads. Little available land. High crime, divorce and suicide rates. Exorbitant prices for necessities. Limited recreational possibilities. Who on earth would want to live here?

About 60,000 people. With just about that many reasons why.

They'll tell you they're the last of the real individualists—or that they're just plain crazy. They'll say that they're inlanders, but that's all they have in common. Or maybe they'll explain that it's the Interior's severe weather that makes people here different. One way or another, they *will* tell you that they're different—not only from other Alaskans, but from everybody else everywhere. Except for those who'll disagree with everything that's just been said, and who'll explain just how wonderful and friendly people can be despite stressful environments, thereby proving what they set out to disprove: that here are 60,000 people spread out over several hundred thousand square miles, each with a special perspective on life in the Interior.

There are, in any case, several constants in this discussion. We'll start with the weather. It's colder than southern Alaska in winter, warmer in summer than the northern part of the state. Translate this meteorological schizophrenia into human terms, and you have the sadomasochistic theory of life in the Interior: to live here, you have to like to suffer or to watch others suffer, preferably both. A similar climatic hypothesis claims that extremes of weather breed extremes in human behavior, that gritting your teeth through months of sub-zero darkness, then erupting into delirious sunshine, creates unfillable grooves in the psyche, rendering you unfit for life in moderate climes. All this is necessarily unprovable, but notice that Fairbanks is the only community in Alaska that marks each of the year's turnings with a festival: Summer and Winter Solstice fairs, the Winter Carnival on the spring equinox, and the fall Equinox Marathon. These dates are important; they mean your life is about to change.

Interior Alaskans offer a variety of self-evaluations: the "rugged individualist" school of thought, which claims that only the hardiest, most independent people can live in such a rough land; and the "mixed nut" theory, which contends that only those who can't get along anywhere else would flee to the end of the road—that Interior Alaska is either America's escape valve or an open-air mental ward. And Fairbanks legislator Brian Rogers thinks he's got the definitive word on these folks. "In the Alaska Public Forum survey of 1976, the majority of people here, on the majority of questions about public policy, when offered a list of solutions and 'other,' marked 'other.' Everyone's got their own solution . . ."

So much for impressions. Let's look at some facts about this particular 18% of Alaska's population. Approximately one-fifth of the residents are Alaska Natives, either Athabascan Indian or Eskimo; another fifth are military personnel and their dependents. The remainder are predominantly white Americans; several thousand blacks live here, too, mostly in Fairbanks or on military installations. There is, as well, an indeterminately large immigrant community of South Americans, Asians and Europeans. Perhaps one-third of the non-Native population has arrived within the past five years.

Opposite
Dee Olin is the youthful mayor of Ruby, a one-time gold rush town that has settled into a new, steadier existence. Here, the mayor washes clothes on the porch of her log cabin.
(Betsy Hart)

Below
Dr. William Wood, former president of the University of Alaska, entered politics a few years ago and today is the mayor of Fairbanks.
(Robert Langlotz)

Studies have debunked the image of the Interior Alaskan as a rugged individualist leading a rustic, woodsy life. It turns out, you see, that only 6% of the people in the North Star Borough live without running water; only 2% want to live without central heating.

Fairbanks relies on two military bases—Fort Wainwright (where this photo was taken) and Eielson Air Force Base—although the number of military personnel stationed in the area has declined in recent years.
(Robert Langlotz)

All but 15% of the people here are under 45; half are under 25. There are proportionately more men than women compared to the national average, in which women are the majority sex; here men hold a small numerical advantage. Average income is about $13,000 a year, but there are extremes of income included in that average, from the less-than-$5,000 of an impoverished village family to the more-than-$50,000 of a university scientist.

Most people in the Interior live in or near Fairbanks. The North Star Borough accounts for about 56,000 of the Interior's 60,000 residents. There is ground transportation to only a handful of the Interior's communities—almost 10,000 people can travel to their homes only by air and, in some cases and some seasons, riverboat.

Diverse as Interior Alaskans are, they have some interesting things in common. For one thing, they're more liable than anyone else in America to be seasonally employed. "Fairbanks sees more seasonal

employment than the rest of Alaska—and more than the rest of the United States," points out Lottie Fleeks of the Alaska Unemployment Office in Fairbanks. And if the Fairbanks work force labors only seasonally, the situation is even more extreme outside the urban center.

In addition, Interior Alaskans travel frequently—and not only to warmer spots during the winter. "You have to be mobile to get here," Kathy Rogers, a travel agent in Fairbanks, notes of her clients. And she notices that they take an "individualistic" approach to travel. "Interior Alaskans have strenuously avoided group travel," she remarks. "Of course our age profile up here is young, and young people tend to be more adventurous, more willing to do the untypical."

Finally, Interior people suffer from a curious interplay of environmental and emotional factors summed up this way by psychologist Mike Graff of Tanana Chiefs Conference: "People get depressed everywhere. But nobody freezes to death in Mazatlan." Bitter weather and winter darkness combine with isolation to produce an undeniably stressful environment—when you haven't seen the sun for weeks and your car's battery is dead and your plumbing is frozen, and then your spouse gets drunk after losing the only job around, it can all be too much. And unfortunately help—professional or family—is often distant when such a crisis occurs.

Annually, Interior Alaska sees a rash of suicides, household breakups, child abuse, and other evidences of emotional disorder. But this doesn't happen in the middle of winter, as you might expect, explains Paul Pesika of the Center for Family Therapy. "The cabin fever breakout comes when the sun is coming out. People have held on till then, and then their problems don't go away even though the weather gets better. Problems tend to be bunched into that time period."

The severity of the problems that explode during this "bunching period" may color people's perceptions of their environment, for although statistically Interior Alaskans are no crazier or more violent than anyone else in the state, our own self-image tends to be that "you don't have to be crazy to live here, but it helps." We're self-defined heroes in some strange struggle between the human spirit and the devastations of isolation, darkness and cold. If not heroes—well then, survivors, almost the same thing.

And this myth may, finally, be what really distinguishes people of Interior Alaska, indicates University of Alaska statistician Jack Kruse. His studies have debunked the image of the Interior Alaskan as a rugged individualist leading a rustic, woodsy life. It turns out, you see, that only 6% of the people in the North Star Borough live without running water; only 2% want to live without central heating. And what about the 200-plus civic organizations—from Beekeepers to Alaska Studebaker Owners—that cram the booklet on civic organizations put out in this alleged hotbed of self-sufficiency?

"The typical Fairbanksan lives in Island Homes or another suburban subdivision," Kruse says, "because

what is 'typical' is whatever is done by the bulk of the people." Then why is the atypical individualist held up as the norm? "The fact that we have such a myth about ourselves may be what really makes us different. A community, after all, is not just the sum of its parts, but consists of the diverse acts and feelings of people. There will always be those who contribute more than their fair share to the community identity. Here, it seems that they tend to be extremists, and the extremes tend to be "further out" from the average than in other places.

So an Interior Alaskan could as easily live in a split-

Chuck Reese, proprietor of the South Fairbanks Industrial Park, calls his city "the most natural sleeping beauty you've ever seen . . . just waiting for the crown prince to give it a little kiss . . ."
(Jane Pender)

Above
Sammy Sam, oldest resident of Huslia, agrees to have his photo taken outside his cabin. Huslia is on the Koyukuk River, near the western edge of Alaska's Interior country.
(Matthew Donohoe)

Left
Gary Urman, principal of the Koyukuk school, rings a traditional brass bell to draw youngsters into the classroom.
(Matthew Donohoe)

John Eubank spearheaded a drive to bring volunteer fire protection to the rural area where he lives. An anti-government campaigner, Eubank ran for North Star Borough mayor in 1976 on the "BLAP" platform— "Bloodsuckers, Leeches and Parasites," his summary description of government officials. (Charlotte Casey, Staff)

level home in suburban Westgate as in a kerosene-lit cabin-cum-outhouse in Chicken. From illegal aliens working as dishwashers for cash only, to village-born Athabascan executives, to members of back-to-the-land communes . . . we're all here, rubbing shoulders and exchanging opinions with varying levels of tolerance for each other.

And because diversity is ultimately the touchstone of living in the Interior, here are glimpses of a few of the individuals you'll find in the inland heart of Alaska. We don't offer them as "representative"—that would take at least 60,000 pages.

JOHN EUBANK

He is a direct descendant of one of the signers of the Declaration of Independence and of Davy Crockett as well. He came to Fairbanks 18 years ago with no clear intention of staying, got in a fight with

the government and stayed on "out of spite. They gave me hell. I'll give them hell back."

John Eubank is anti-government. Not just big government: any government. The way he sees it, people came to Alaska so they wouldn't have to live with restrictions on everything. "You'd be free to live your own lifestyle without interference by your neighbors. So what if you didn't have water and sewage furnished—I thought that's what we all came up here to get away from."

He's drinking coffee in his living room as he describes the fight he's waged to stay on this five-acre homesite, now just five minutes from the Fairbanks airport but close to nothing when he moved here. The cluttered walls are decked with abstract pictures painted on boards, old photographs, a sign that says, "Sailors Have More Fun." A fireman's badge from the Chena Goldstream Volunteers lies on the table.

Twenty years ago there wasn't anyone else on this section of the Nenana Highway. "It was unreserved and unappropriated federal land," Eubank points out, overlooked by a Fairbanks corporation when it bought the remaining parcels in the area. Eubank got clearance from the Bureau of Land Management to live on the parcel, then tried to get title to the homesite.

"The state tried to get us off," he says. "The state wants to get every inch of land possible. They stake claims on paper and then try to claim anything they've missed." It took him 10 years—"what with the BLM dragging their feet, and then the Land Claims"— but he did get title to the land.

In the meantime he'd moved a trailer onto the property and begun to erect a wannigan next to it. The wannigan was so large it dwarfed the trailer, and Eubank decided to enclose the whole unit with another building—in effect, forming a wide enclosed porch around the entire structure. "Saves heat, too," he says smugly.

While building up his homesite, Eubank has continued his campaign against government erosion of what he sees as the "Alaskan right" to an unhampered style of living. In 1976 he ran for North Star

Borough mayor on the "BLAP" platform. That stands for "Bloodsuckers, Leeches and Parasites," his summary description of government officials.

"They ought to leave the people alone," he maintains. "It used to be that everyone resolved problems among themselves. Now the government encourages people to argue among themselves by giving them a chance to complain in public."

That people will take care of their own needs without government "help" is proved to Eubank by the organization, over the last few years, of a volunteer fire department in his area.

"We have two volunteer EMTs [emergency medical technicians]," he says with pride, "and 20 badges assigned. Actually we've had more sign up and we'll issue badges as soon as we can afford to buy some."

Eubank thinks life has changed in Interior Alaska and finds it not to his liking. But he's determined to stay here and fight to see what's left of what he calls "Alaskans' rights" protected. "I'm gonna tough it out. I'm gonna fight government as long as I live. The only thing I can see to do is to try to make life better."

MEGAN LEARY

"Well," Megan Leary says, settling back with a cigarette, "there are two versions of how I got to Alaska. Do you want the blustery version or the touchy-feely version?"

She's just driven in from Ferry, a little settlement near Mount McKinley National Park, where she lives across a treacherous railroad bridge in a single-room cabin, and where this city girl who spent her life in New York and San Francisco is learning to fish and hunt and garden. She's driven in her truck with her two dogs to put in two and a half days this week as an advocate at the Women in Crisis emergency shelter for battered women.

"Some people think it's a crazy combination," she says comfortably. "I think of it as a good balance."

So, how did she get here? "Well the official Alaska version is that I came up here on a two-week vacation

For many residents of the Interior, a successful trapping season means food for the cache, skins for clothing, and furs to sell for cash or barter for needed items. For Pete Buist, president of the Interior Alaska Trappers Association and the Alaska Wildlife Federation, trapping is a way of life.

Clockwise from above
► Pete Buist patrols his trapline, hoping for a good catch of spring beaver. The sticks he is carrying are bait to lure the beaver to his trap.
► Bringing home the beaver.
► Buist uses a draw knife to remove all fat and flesh from the pelt.
► Pete at his cabin on Chena Ridge Road examines the beaver pelt.
(All photos by Tom Walker)

117

Megan Leary, one-time city girl, lives in a one-room cabin at Ferry, near Mount McKinley National Park, surrounded by trappers and miners. Abandoning a stock-exchange job in San Francisco, Megan headed for Interior Alaska in 1976 and within weeks was working as a sheetrock taper, dishwasher, waitress and janitor. When she moved from San Francisco to Ferry to take up a bush lifestyle she was not overly prepared: "I'd never seen a gun except on TV . . . (and) when I first got down there I didn't even know how to build a fire!" (Charlotte Casey, Staff)

and never left. The unofficial version is that I'd been working at Pacific Stock Exchange in downtown San Francisco, commuting every day, feeling my life go nowhere."

She arrived in early summer, 1976. Almost immediately, in that boom year, she was offered a job. "So for the first two weeks I thought Alaska was made up of angles—I was working as a sheetrock taper. I'd never heard of sheetrock before and I thought that taper meant to go to a point." She stuck it out till the company went bankrupt. "I decided not to work for the pipeline, so I started doing day labor. One day I was sent out to a local restaurant to do some outdoor work. I only went because the job said 'lunch included,' and I was broke enough that that meant something." The management found her a diligent worker and asked her to stay on, and she spent the winter doing everything from dishwashing to waiting tables to swamping in the evenings.

Then she went back to New York to visit her family, drove back to California and "flew up here to finish off some business," intending to move back to California. "I thought I'd done my Alaska thing, that it really wasn't for me. I've been here ever since."

She met a woman who owned a homestead in Ferry and who offered to let her live there if she'd fix the place up. "Let's see: I've got a frame cabin with no insulation and an A-frame cabin with no roof. When I moved in, I got right to work, painted the trim on the frame cabin and planted marigolds."

She was not overly prepared for rural living. "I'd never seen a gun except on TV—now I've learned to shoot. But those first weeks! I was petrified. So I bought a puppy—a two-month old puppy to protect me! He was more scared than I was." She chuckles constantly as she recalls her introduction to the community. "Rumor got around that here was this girl from New York. The old-timers would sort of go by the place and watch. Then one day one of them stopped in, and I handed him a beer, and after that they were terrific to me."

She continues to live alone, and enjoys her relationships with the trappers and miners of the area.

"It's a really neat exchange, a sharing. I'm a woman who's really different than any they've known. And I'm learning all sorts of things about outdoor living—when I first got down there I didn't even know how to build a fire!"

JUNE AND MARILYNN FORREST

June Forrest's new apartment in Fairbanks' senior citizen's complex isn't yet ready for luncheon guests, and her daughter-in-law Marilynn is on a deadline for a research contract, so they meet this Friday for a quick bite at a downtown cafeteria. Marilynn arrives early, mock-complaining about her clothes "just hanging off me" since the arrival of her first child, and dives for the coconut cream pie. She waves energetically when June arrives.

Both are enthusiastic migrants from other states—June from Michigan, Marilynn from Minnesota. Both came to Alaska alone and found themselves trailed by family—June by her sons, Marilynn by her sisters. Now the combined "family"—counting permanent roommates and assorted ex's—comes to a dozen or so, and all within a decade.

June arrived in midwinter, 1969, for a job interview. "I got off the plane in Stateside clothes and trailed across the tarmac without boots. I couldn't even see the town for the ice fog, but I decided to explore. I saw Two Street—sedate in those days—and the library, since I'd met the librarian on the plane. Everyone was helpful. I guess they knew from my clothes that I was new. A cabbie took me around the whole town for five bucks. I was sold."

She took the job. "I went home and sold everything. When I came back I needed some decent clothes, so I went to Penney's for material for a parky. Everyone got together to advise me. It was a real coffee klatch. I was at home within three weeks."

"But then," she shrugs, "I'm a doer, a joiner. And you can really get involved here—all you have to do is open your mouth."

She drags on her cigarette momentously. "And that," she nods, "is how I got into theater." A hearty chuckle. "Now you be sure to mention this—that I came up here with no experience and have been playing a whore for 10 years." She refers to her annual appearance as an over-the-hill hooker in the town's summer melodrama entitled, with the passing years, *Oil Can Annie*, *Pipeline Fanny* and (currently) *Gasline Gladys.*

Marilynn Forrest, who married June's son Jack in a midwinter candle-lit-ceremony under the trees at the Public Library, is similarly enthusiastic about her adoptive town. Like June, who came from Detroit, she came from a large city—in her case, Minneapolis. Fairbanks offered her an experience of small-town life that she relishes.

Marilynn arrived on the afternoon of the 1976 summer solstice. "I had no concept of what the town would be like, although I had a preconceived notion of the kind of people who would be here—not really the lifestyle, but the fact that the people would be full of spirit. Fairbanks had a national stereotype as being rustic, a boom town, a place of hardy spirits."

And indeed, the first evening, she was not disappointed. "The people were certainly full of spirits. And good as gold. I thought, if people can be this helpful right in the middle of a boom, when things are so adverse, think of how they'd be in more normal times."

Coming to the state with experience in journalism and government, Marilynn was not overanxious about finding employment, opting instead to wait until "I could settle in, make contacts. I saw that the potential for upward mobility was incredible. You can really mold your job into what you want to do, or find just the job to suit you." She worked as a researcher for the North Star Borough until she felt confident enough to launch out into independent consulting work, which she finds particularly suitable to her new duties as a mother.

"You can do just about anything here," she emphasizes. "Coming to Fairbanks is an adventure. It's always exciting. There's always going to be something popping out of the bushes at you."

Marilynn Forrest feeds the youngest of her family.
(Debbie Miller)

Below
Angela Huntington blesses food about to be served during an Athabascan potlatch at Galena. Potlatches are often held to honor those who have died recently in a village or region.
(Betsy Hart)

Bottom
For many villages, July 4 marks the biggest community celebration of the year, with parades, picnics, games, races and other traditional Fourth of July events.
Matthew Shelborne, 27 months, rides a patriotic tricycle during a fourth of July parade at McGrath.
(Alissa Crandall)

Above
A game of pan poker at Koyukuk. The locals here have a name for the game which translates as "killing time." From left are Sally Pilot, Martha Nelson, Arthur Malamute and Amelia Nelson. Many villages have one building that is known as the pan house, and games often can be found there during long winter months.
(Matthew Donohoe)

Left
Audrey Tritt, princess of the annual Arctic Village spring carnival, models a dress made by her mother, Margaret, from hand-tanned caribou skin. Audrey's slippers are also from caribou skin, with fox trim and intricate Athabascan beadwork.
(Dennis and Debbie Miller)

JESSICA AND ROBERT BITTNER

"Wanna see my room?" Nonny demands, pulling at a visitor's sweater with the 6-year-old version of a rhetorical question. We follow her upstairs.

Born in bush Alaska, Nonny's never lived in such spacious surroundings. "Here is my bed, and there's Moss's, and there's little Willow's, she narrates, and leads on to the desk, and her drawings, and the play ladder . . .

Downstairs, Jessica Bittner is making tea, newborn Willow on her hip. Robert, just home from work on a nearby road job, is finishing dinner and opening a beer.

The Bittners live about 30 miles outside Fairbanks on what Jessica terms a "homestead." Robert instantly disagrees with the terminology, calling it "a basic economic fallacy. Homestead! The word should be used only for free land. Hell, people use it for anyone with one acre and a chicken." He says it's "a sore point," that he's somewhat bitter that he had to purchase his land, that he was still a child when real homesteading ended in Alaska.

But Robert has no other term for his establishment with its unfinished house, greenhouses, outbuildings, gardens and meadows. Homesite? Farmstead? Ranch? Robert has a point, but "homestead" still seems appropriate, describing a way of life, not just something from economic-political history.

The Bittners began developing their place four years ago when, as Robert says, "I didn't trust the employment picture to be stable, so I wanted to get enough things going to meet my basic needs. I wanted to spend less money on necessities and more money on increasing my net worth." He found five acres, worked to pay off the land, and started to build.

Nonny offers a guided tour of the place. The greenhouse is new, full of tomatoes with a few squash stuffed in a corner. The garden is half an acre, with a huge potato patch and lots of cabbages, beans and peas. Nonny has her own garden, neat little rows of wild camomile.

Above
Jessica Bittner with newborn Willow in the kitchen area of the family's uncompleted rural home. The Bittners are growing proficient at living on less and becoming more independent. "I just like to raise animals and grow gardens," says Jessica. "I like to handle my own survival."
(Charlotte Casey, Staff)

Left
Moss Bittner and the original cabin which became the chicken coop and workshed.
(Charlotte Casey, Staff)

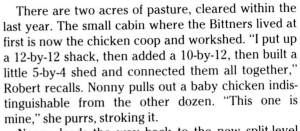

Clockwise from right

► Bill Ruth skis on overflow ice on the East Fork Chandalar River during a cross-country expedition in the Brooks Range. (Johnny Johnson)

► Backpacking, especially in the Brooks Range, is becoming a popular activity in the Interior. Dave Cohen relaxes in the tundra near the John River, in Gates of the Arctic National Monument. (Jim Shives)

► Margaret Tritt drags a heavy load of firewood back to Arctic Village behind her snow machine. (Dennis and Debbie Miller)

► Hunters load equipment aboard a DeHavilland Beaver floatplane in the Koyukuk River, at the village of Bettles Field. Their destination was a remote hunting camp in the Brooks Range—a favorite spot for hunters, backpackers and Interior wildlife. (Gil Mull)

► Eagle residents Jim Scott and Micki Harmon run their freight canoe up the Yukon River. The river is a year-round highway for residents, who travel by boat in the summer, and snow machine, skis and dog sled in the winter. (Nancy Simmerman)

There are two acres of pasture, cleared within the last year. The small cabin where the Bittners lived at first is now the chicken coop and workshed. "I put up a 12-by-12 shack, then added a 10-by-12, then built a little 5-by-4 shed and connected them all together," Robert recalls. Nonny pulls out a baby chicken indistinguishable from the other dozen. "This one is mine," she purrs, stroking it.

Nonny leads the way back to the new split-level home that Robert started two years ago, passing a dozen sheds including an ingenious two-story detached shower and an old state fair booth. "I started by building the root cellar," he says after settling downstairs next to the fire, "and then dug out this section by hand." He then built the four-level structure that he's still working on, finishing off sections as he gets the cash. Everything is paid for. One day this will be a comfortable suburban home, and Robert plans to make a tidy profit.

In one sense, this certainly is not a homestead, but an investment, for Robert doesn't view this as a permanent home, the place their children will inherit. "Ideally, I'd like to have the money to buy more lots and build more houses. This, right now, helps us financially. We grow our own potatoes so we don't have to spend a dollar on Rice-a-Roni."

"A dollar!" Jess snorts. "It's more like three these days." She is proud to claim a grocery bill of $20 each week for the five-member family, explaining that the gardens and animals provide the rest of their food. For Jessica, who's lived in rural Alaska for more than seven years, there are more than economic advantages to living as they do.

"I just like to raise animals and grow gardens. I like to handle my own survival. Also I'm staying home with three kids, and now's the time to get proficient at these basic skills." She admits to a failure in the chicken department this year, for she lost a dozen chicks when the temperature dropped. But she won't let that happen again. Each year she increases her knowledge of how to provide for herself and her family.

But Robert dismisses as "romantic" the idea that a

family can meet all their needs from such a homestead. "You can't make it on five acres," he shakes his head, "and we really haven't got enough space to raise a cash crop."

"Tomatoes?" Jessica offers cautiously. "In greenhouses?" He grins at her.

TERI VIERICK

The back entrance to Teri Vierick's property is blocked by a new electrified fence; the old pigyard has been changed into a pasture for Misty, Sharon Vierick's tawny mare. The new patch cuts up to the two-story log home, past a huge garden and greenhouse, near a little barn. Even from the bottom of the hill you can see Teri doing yoga on the porch.

The five acres where the Viericks annually raise much of the food their family consumes looks like a well-organized subsistence farm in rural Alaska. But it's within walking distance of the University of Alaska, in an area thickly settled with the community's intellectual and political notables: environmentalist Celia Hunter, artist Ron Senungetuk, poet David Stark. And it's within shouting distance of the cabin where, at a party a quarter of a century ago, Smith college biology graduate Teri Norton met another scientist—Les Vierick, then a local celebrity for a daring rescue on Mount McKinley.

Teri came to Alaska, she grins, "instead of going to Mexico," and immediately fell in love with the country. Intent upon making a life here, she returned to Smith to finish her master's degree. The next year she married Les Vierick and for three years afterward they drove the Alaska Highway every summer. "We brought our food with us from dried-food supply houses, spent the time out in the mountains away from cities, and ate all the wild fresh food we could find." Wintertimes, they each finished doctoral degrees at the University of Colorado. Teri's dissertation was on mammal adaptation to cold climates, and she applied her skills to teaching and research at the University of Alaska after the Viericks moved here.

But three children and less than a decade later, Teri left academic science to embark, as she explains, on an odyssey that has since led into Sufi dancing, yoga, herbal medicine and the use of music as a meditative discipline. Not that she's left teaching—she shakes her blond head—for her classes in wild plant gathering and tai chi are staple offerings at Tanana Valley Community College. "In my spare time," she smiles, she practices for the Pearl Creek Recorder Consort, a semi-professional group that plays baroque and renaissance music.

The mosquitoes become too much and Teri retreats to the house through a handsome living room with hand-pegged wooden floor, down a narrow spiral staircase, to the sauna, which has been heating all afternoon. After relaxing there awhile she serves a light lunch of yogurt and rose-petal jam, and brings out the notebook of information she's been gathering for an intended book on edible and medicinal plants of the Interior. Her academic training shows: every

Above
Steve DuBois ages large cuts of moose in his Fairbanks garage—more than 600 pounds' worth. Many residents of the Interior rely on hunting for meat, especially moose meat.
(Dave Johnson)

Left
Teri Vierick practices yoga on the front porch of her cabin near Fairbanks.
(Debbie Miller)

123

Lower left
Tom Caesar removes membranes from chum salmon roe in a Tanana processing plant.
(Len Sherwin)

Below
Bessy Wholecheese pulls lush (a cod-like fish) from the Yukon River in the Galena area. The temperature was about 10 below with a breeze that further lowered the temperature, but Bessy—a lifelong resident of Galena who has trapped and subsistence-hunted for most of her life—didn't seem to mind.
(Matthew Donohoe)

Right
Altona Brown, known along the Yukon River as a great seamstress and trapper, prepares food for her dogs in Ruby. She and her late husband had one of the biggest commercial fishing camps on the Yukon.
(Matthew Donohoe)

reference is noted, every plant filed under its botanical name.

She explains why she—who still tells anecdotes from her party-going years—has used no alcohol or drugs for several years. "Such things can change one's consciousness temporarily, but yoga practices are designed to accomplish the same purpose more safely and with more enduring results." She's excited by an upcoming visit to the Omega Institute in New York, where she plans to study the relationship of music and mysticism. She recalls that "Picasso once said that he spent 60 years trying to learn to draw like a child. I've studied science, practiced sports, played music, sought for wisdom, and think I have finally reached nowhere at the age of 48."

GINO FIELDS

It is a quiet afternoon in the Persian Room, but it won't be long before the evening traffic arrives. Gino is cleaning glasses and wiping off the bar. Eugene Fields admits that "Gino" isn't the most typical name for an Athabascan bartender.

He likes the view through the big front windows out to Second Avenue, a few years ago notorious as boomtown Fairbanks's "Two Street." When business is really dead, he can sit at one of the windowside tables and watch the downtown pedestrians. He likes his job. He likes his life, he says. "I'm a content person."

Where is he from? "Fairbanks, but raised in Fort Yukon. It depends on who asks me that. If you ask, I say I'm from Fairbanks. If you're from the village, I say I'm from Fort Yukon."

He has only the happiest recollections of boyhood in the village. "When I was a kid I couldn't find anything wrong with the place, the hunting, the village people. Now I'm older, more educated. I don't go down to the village so often, but if you ask me, I'll say I would like to live there best."

Jobs keep him in Fairbanks and his friends are here. He's worked in several places on Second

Avenue, feels he's done well. "I've made a lot a money and thrown it all away."

A woman wants to play the juke box and asks for change in Kutchin. Gino answers in the same language and they joke a bit.

"That's a real advantage in a Native bar," he says after he waits on a few new arrivals. "I speak the language. As a matter of fact, my best qualification as a bartender is being a Native."

Gino tells me he is working on a book, that he's taken writing courses and has a good section already done. He thinks that not enough information is available on rape prevention, and he has a daughter. He's very concerned about the problem and has done massive research. "I should get back to work on that."

The evening crowd is arriving. Irene Mary Sherman walks in with a bunch of Native youngsters, arrayed as usual in her collection of historical political buttons and carrying her personalized beer mug. "Hey, kid!" she yells at Gino. He gets back to work.
—Pat Monaghan

Gino Fields, Athabascan bartender in the Persian Room on Two Street. Born in Fort Yukon, he enjoys his work in Fairbanks. "There's a real advantage in a Native bar," he says. "I speak the language. As a matter of fact, my best qualification as a bartender is being a Native." (Charlotte Casey, Staff)

125

Gil Mull

Interior Alaskans offer a variety of self-evaluations: the "rugged individualist" school of thought, which claims that only the hardiest, most independent people can live in such a rough land; and the "mixed nut" theory, which contends that only those who can't get along anywhere else would flee to the end of the road—that Interior Alaska is either America's escape valve or an open-air mental ward . . .

Betsy Hart

Dave Johnson

Betsy Hart

Matthew Donohoe

Ed Cooper

Alissa Crandall

Tom Walker

Charlotte Casey, Staff

Charlotte Casey, Staff

127

ALASKA GEOGRAPHIC® back issues

ALL PRICES SUBJECT TO CHANGE.

Your $39 membership in The Alaska Geographic Society includes four subsequent issues of ALASKA GEOGRAPHIC®, the Society's official quarterly. Please add $4 for non-U.S. memberships.

Additional membership information is available upon request. Single copies of the ALASKA GEOGRAPHIC® back issues are also available. When ordering, please make payments in U.S. funds and add $1.50 postage/handling per copy. Non-U.S. postage extra. To order back issues send your check or money order and volumes desired to:

The Alaska Geographic Society

P.O. Box 93370, Anchorage, AK 99509